Emotions Anonymous

INTRODUCTION TO THE TWELVE-STEP PROGRAM OF EMOTIONS ANONYMOUS®

EMOTIONS ANONYMOUS® was formed by a group of individuals who found a New Way of Life by working the Twelve-Step Program of Alcoholics Anonymous, as adapted for people with emotional problems.

We invite you to discover, as we have, that our EA fellowship of weekly meetings is warm and friendly, and that it is also important in achieving and maintaining emotional health.

The Twelve Suggested Steps and The Twelve Traditions are our guides for our meetings and for living one day at a time because ours is a Twenty-Four Hour Program.

EMOTIONS ANONYMOUS® is a nonprofit organization, supported by the voluntary contributions of its members.

We thank Alcoholics Anonymous for their permission to use this Program — and we thank God *as we understand Him.*

God, grant me the serenity
To accept the things I cannot change
Courage to change the things I can
And the wisdom to know the difference.

Emotions Anonymous

EMOTIONS ANONYMOUS INTERNATIONAL

SAINT PAUL, MINNESOTA

1978

— Published by: —
EMOTIONS ANONYMOUS INTERNATIONAL
P.O. Box 4245
St. Paul, Minnesota 55104
Phone (612) 647-9712

First Printing	1978
Second Printing	1980
Third Printing	1981
Fourth Printing	1983
Fifth Printing	1984
Sixth Printing	1984
Seventh Printing	1985
Eighth Printing	1986
Ninth Printing	1987 (Revised)
Tenth Printing	1988
Eleventh Printing	1989
Twelfth Printing	1990

Library of Congress Catalog Card Number: RA790.A1E5633
ISBN: 0-9607356-0-7

CONTENTS

vi

APPENDICES

CHAPTER I

HOW IT STARTED

Emotions Anonymous was started on July 6, 1971, in St. Paul, Minnesota by a group of people who during the previous five years had been members of another Twelve-Step Program. Some of the recovery stories in this book have been written by these people.

We chose the name "EMOTIONS ANONYMOUS" and Alcoholics Anonymous granted us permission to use their Twelve Steps and Twelve Traditions adapted for persons with emotional problems. A Trusted Servants Temporary Committee was formed, elected by the membership, which became our International Service Board of Trustees.

Emotions Anonymous has grown rapidly in the past six years. At this time approximately 200 chapters have been established in the United States, Canada, Mexico, Germany, Switzerland, and Finland.* We believe our growth is largely the result of a real effort to follow, as closely as possible, the Twelve Traditions as originally written by Alcoholics Anonymous.

We have had good relationships with doctors, psychiatrists, psychologists, counselors, clergymen, and other professionals. Many of them refer their patients, clients, or parishioners to Emotions Anonymous, for which we are grateful.

It is our hope that those of you who have as yet found no help for your emotional problems may begin to find the answer in this book and join us in our search for serenity.

1

---

*As of 1988, there are over 1,500 groups worldwide.

CHAPTER II

INTRODUCTION

EMOTIONS ANONYMOUS is a fellowship of persons who share their experiences, their strengths, their weaknesses, feelings, and their hopes with one another to solve their emotional problems and/or to learn to live at peace with unsolved problems. We come to EA to learn to live a new way of life through the Twelve-Step Program.

The only requirement for membership in our fellowship is an honest desire to become emotionally well and healthy.

No dues or fees are required. EA is supported by contributions from its members, but this is not a requirement for membership.

Because we are anonymous, only first names are used at meetings and at the level of press, radio, and television.

Emotions Anonymous is a spiritual Program; it is not a religious Program. The Steps suggest a belief in a Power greater than ourselves, "God as we understand Him." The Program does not attempt to tell us what our Higher Power must be. It can be whatever we choose, for example, human love, a force for good, the group itself, nature, the universe, or the traditional God (Deity). Persons of all faiths or persons with no identifiable Higher Power become members. Persons who have lost faith in a Higher Power, in other persons, and in themselves become members.

We never discuss religion, politics, national, or international issues or other belief systems or policies. EA has no opinion on outside issues.

We have discovered that we are not unique in our difficulties and illnesses and we need never feel "alone" again.

Emotions Anonymous is non-professional. Emotional

illness affects persons of all ages and from all walks of life. Everyone practices our Twelve-Step Program as an individual, for himself or herself, and not for another person.

Each person is entitled to his or her own opinions and may express them (within the precepts of EA) at meetings. We are all equal - no one is more important than another.

We utilize the Twelve Steps and Twelve Traditions of Alcoholics Anonymous, adapted with the permission of Alcoholics Anonymous World Services, Inc., for persons with emotional problems.

The Twelve Suggested Steps of Emotions Anonymous are written in the past tense because they are a report of actions already taken, attitudes learned, and feelings expressed which through personal experience have brought recovery to thousands of persons with emotional problems. The Twelve Steps say, "This is what we did to become well."

The Twelve Steps are goals toward which we work and the measuring sticks by which we estimate our progress. The important thing is that we try each day, a day at a time, to practice the Steps to the best of our ability and as honestly as we can because ours is a Twenty-Four Hour Program.

Anyone is welcome in EA. Emotional illness does not discriminate because of age, sex, religion, race, income or occupation. There is no degree of illness that qualifies a person for membership. We may have been hospitalized or found ourselves dependent on pills, or we may have come to the Program only because life was uncomfortable and we were looking for a better way. The symptoms that led us to seek help are varied - depression, inability to cope with reality, personal problems, or psychosomatic ailments are just a few. If you feel that your symptoms may be caused by some physical ailment, we urge you to have a medical examination to reassure yourself. Do not assume that all physical ailments or symptoms are caused by emotions, although every day we hear the opinions of professionals, including persons in medicine, who believe from their own experience that many physical illnesses are caused by emotions.

At meetings we learn that symptoms and backgrounds do not matter. We do not judge what anyone has done in the past. We find love and acceptance all around us. Being accepted by others may be the beginning of our learning to accept ourselves.

The first Step states, "We admitted that we were powerless over our emotions - that our lives had become unmanageable." Since we do not diagnose, judge, or give advice on personal or family matters (Concept Four), it is the privilege of each EA member to determine for himself the degree of his powerlessness over his emotions. No other person can - nor does he or she have the right to - judge just how powerless another person is.

As we listen to what other members have to say at meetings, we begin to discover things about ourselves. We are amazed to hear people describe the very feelings we thought were unique in ourselves, but as time goes on we lose our astonishment, for we begin to realize how much like others we are. We are not alone. We begin to act upon the knowledge we gain and attempt to make changes in our lives which will bring us closer to emotional well-being.

The Program does not work overnight. It has usually taken us many years to reach the point of turning to EA for help. We cannot expect immediate results. At first we may have to settle for the glimmer of hope that comes from seeing others who have been where we are and have found help. Then, as we begin to practice the Twelve Steps, we find that our lives begin to change. As we grow in the Program we experience a peace not known before.

"If your life is like a shoe that pinches," if you are just not as happy as you would like to be, or if you have gone the whole route of other methods of treatment and have not achieved inner peace and serenity, we invite you to read this book wherein some of us share our experiences - how we once were and how we are today after practicing and living each day, a day at a time, to the best of our ability, the Twelve-Step Program of Emotions Anonymous.

We invite you to attend our weekly meetings which are warm and friendly and which are so important in achieving and maintaining emotional health.

We believe you may be interested in some comments from a few professionals about the Emotions Anonymous Program. Chapter Three contains some of their thoughts.

CHAPTER III

ENDORSEMENTS

We of Emotions Anonymous believe our readers would be interested in the opinions of several professionals who have observed the suffering of some of our members and have witnessed their recovery and growth through the Twelve-Step Program. This chapter contains endorsements from some of these professionals.

FROM A MINISTER AND
DIRECTOR OF REHABILITATION PROGRAMS

EMOTIONS ANONYMOUS has helped many people who are in need of this disciplined Program for living and the fellowship which supports this Program. The goal of EA has been to help people live as comfortably as possible inside their own skin. There isn't a single human being alive who could not prosper emotionally from EA and it is with great respect and admiration that I endorse this Program and refer many people to it.

Reverend Philip L. Hansen
Executive Director
Abbott-Northwestern Hospitals
Rehabilitation Programs
Minneapolis, Minnesota

FROM A LUTHERAN MINISTER

After many years of acquaintance with the EA way of life and many visits with persons who are living that life, one day at a time, I am pleased to give the Twelve-Step way of life my hearty endorsement. It is, in my belief and experience, a profound spiritual, if not explicitly religious, expression of the way we are all created to live.

As persons created to live with trust in a caring Creator and with concern for our fellow creatures, we find in the Twelve Steps a way of life which leads us out of futile self-preoccupation and into a living adventure of self-surrender, self-forgetfulness and self-giving. As we lose our lives in this venture of trust and love, we find new strength and purpose for living and experience a joy which seems possible in no other way.

We, at University Lutheran Church of Hope, are grateful that an EA group meets weekly in our building, and as a pastor, I find myself frequently encouraging persons to attend the meetings and to live the EA way of life.

May the publication of this book further extend the healing influence of EA that others, too, may receive and share its gifts of hope, meaning, and joy.

Pastor Lowell O. Erdahl
University Lutheran Church of Hope
Minneapolis, Minnesota

FROM A DOCTOR

How prophetic were the words written as the citation which accompanied the Lasker Award when it was presented to Alcoholics Anonymous in 1951 by the American Public Health Association. The citation read in part, "Historians may one day recognize Alcoholics Anonymous to have been a great venture in social pioneering which forged a new instrument for social action in a new therapy based on the kinship of man's common suffering; one having a vast potential for the myriad other ills of mankind."

Now we have Emotions Anonymous which opens the doorway of the Twelve Steps of recovery to the legions of persons who suffer with emotional illness. This Twelve-Step Program suggests to the emotionally ill person: Fear no more; turn your problems over; know yourself, forgive yourself, change yourself, and make amends; review your life daily; meditate and carry the message to others with emotional ills and practice these principles in all your affairs.

Is this successful? You bet! Where there is a desire to rid oneself of the fears, anxieties, and depressions which are making one's life unmanageable and willingness to follow this Program one day at a time, there is seldom failure.

I have heard many success stories from those who follow this Program. Some were too fearful to leave their homes, others were on the verge of self-destruction, and others suffered from fits of anger and the emotional destruction from alcoholism. They learned that they need fear no more; that help was at hand and indeed it is through a higher power and the fellowship of Emotions Anonymous.

I am quite convinced that the principles of the Twelve-Step Program for recovery, as begun by Bill Wilson and Dr. Bob, are indeed divinely inspired principles, that in some mystical way (similar to the way in which the authors of the Bible were inspired) they were themselves inspired in a creation of the Twelve Steps to recovery.

The world has profited from what was begun in Akron, Ohio in 1935 when Bob and Bill first met. The Twelve-Step

Program of recovery has been applied to the emotional ills of mankind by the members of Emotions Anonymous. Their numerous stories of successful recovery are testimony to the validity of this Program.

M.J. Wegleitner, M.D.
El Paso, Texas

FROM A CHEMICAL DEPENDENCY THERAPIST

As long as there are human beings on this earth, they will experience difficulty adjusting to the constant change taking place daily within themselves and around them. This is not a profound statement, just a simple observation of people and life. This is an observation all of us can make if we just get our minds off ourselves and our own problems long enough to take a look around us.

As I work with people and hear their problems on a daily basis, several messages constantly come across to me. "My problem is worse than anyone's problem," "No one has ever had to go through what I'm going through," or "No one can help me, I just know it."

These are not unique statements from mentally ill people, but simply statements and thoughts that go through all of our minds at one time or another. Before we can begin to solve our emotional problems, we need to get over one of the biggest hurdles: Lack of self confidence. Once this is achieved, motivation will set in.

EA is an organization which can help people to overcome the hurdle of self-doubt and despair which accompany our emotional unrest. EA accomplishes this task in ways that professionals cannot:

1. EA groups are not conducted by professionals in the mental health or medical field. If this does occur it is because the individual is a member of EA and it may be his turn to conduct the meeting.

2. EA offers its members a program of recovery which includes the support of other people experiencing similar problems. This I feel helps remove the fear of change.

3. The Twelve Suggested Steps which members follow on their road to recovery gives them insight and direction into the problem-solving process.

4. EA helps the individual work on four important areas of his life, which I feel is the downfall of

most other therapies which have been used in the past and are still being used to a great extent today. EA helps the individual become aware of the physical, psychological, social, and spiritual aspects of one's life and, therefore, promotes more uniform growth within the individual.

In conclusion, I strongly recommend EA to my clients and friends who have difficulty dealing effectively with their emotions. I have also found EA to be a very beneficial referral for my alcoholic and drug addicted clients, along with their regular AA attendance.

EA is a God-sent Program which can help us complicated people deal more realistically with our emotional upheavals. I need not, nor can I, say any more on the effects EA has had on many individuals' lives. Its track record, like AA's, speaks for itself.

David P. Decker
Senior Chemical Dependency Therapist
Dakota County Mental Health Center
South St. Paul, Minnesota

FROM A PRIEST

It is with a deep feeling of gratitude that I share these few thoughts with those who are striving for personal betterment in their relationship with self, fellow human beings, and God, as they understand Him. It is heart-warming to note the group progress that has occurred in the first few years of Emotions Anonymous.

The basic Steps of this Program offer guidelines for real renewal of physical and mental well-being. It further offers opportunity for spiritual growth and serenity of spirit. We witness individuals, through personal effort and determination, along with group support, seeking guidance in practical daily living. They find solutions through specific application of the basic virtues to the character problems of life.

Growth means change - a ceaseless process of becoming different today from what one was yesterday, and different tomorrow from what one is today. And change comes from strength - and strength comes from God. And God has the strength. It is ours for the asking.

May all who seek this strength through the Program of EA find even greater gifts - the power to love, to be at peace, to find meaning in life, and to be truly joyful. God will change me - if I will let Him.

Rev. Mark F. Mindrup, O.F.M. Conv.
Franciscan Retreats
Prior Lake, Minnesota

FROM A PRIEST AND SPIRITUAL DIRECTOR
OF CALIX INTERNATIONAL

When I first became a member of the fellowship of Alcoholics Anonymous, I was concerned with only one goal, and that was, of course, to obtain help in my struggle with the illness of alcoholism. I thank God and Alcoholics Anonymous daily that I have since enjoyed many years of happy sobriety. However, as I grew in my understanding of the Twelve-Step Program by living it, I became aware of subtle changes taking place in myself which I can describe only as attitudinal. My attitudes began to change drastically. As I tried to analyze what was taking place and why, I became aware of the true significance of the Twelve Steps, not as stages to sobriety, but rather as directives to living. They became a way of life - guidelines to a good life, a full life, a wholesome life, a well balanced life, a mature life, a healthy life, and, therefore, a happy life. I began to see sobriety not as a goal but rather a bonus that was a logical consequence of the new attitudes which the living of the Steps developed. I began to notice that I was constantly using the Steps as the basis of my counseling sessions with people of a variety of difficulties. As a priest I had often been called upon to act as a Father Counselor and Confessor. I still daily ask God's pardon for my lack of insights. If I had ever helped anyone prior to my AA affiliation, I am certain it was only as an instrument of Divine Wisdom and not because of any human qualifications. I still feel very strongly today that our greatest responsibility and our greatest dignity is that God does use even the least of us as instruments of His love and healing power. However, He does expect us to develop, to sharpen, and to use the tools with which He has endowed us. For me, the tools are offered us in the very practical, concise and precise Twelve Steps to healthy living.

Somewhere along the line of my own growth in sanity I became aware of this way of life as an answer to practically all human ailments of an emotional nature. I had, at times, toyed with the idea of adapting the Twelve Steps of recovery to other human problems, particularly of an emotional nature. In my stupidity I envisioned a number of changes as being necessary. Imagine then my surprise and sheer joy when I finally heard of Emotions Anonymous. And marvel of marvels, it was adopted with the change of only one word. This gave me a little food for additional self-inventory for I saw myself as still playing God and trying to improve His work. I truly believe that the Twelve-Step Program is a Twentieth Century revelation of the Holy Spirit to counteract the emotional problems which our present pace of living is producing in almost plague-like proportions.

Since I became acquainted with EA I have had numerous contacts with its members, both in helping to interpret and adapt the Steps to life and as a Fifth Step person. I have seen some beautiful, even miraculous successes. It has proven it will work. But, as in AA, it will be successful only in the measure in which it is lived. Take nothing for granted, follow the Steps religiously, be painfully honest with yourself, your God, and with others and you, too, will begin to experience something beautiful happening to you. The Program doesn't promise a life free from pain or problems but it does promise a life of peace, serenity, and happiness in spite of the pains of normal, human living.

Reverend Arnold Luger
Spiritual Director of Calix International
Minneapolis, Minnesota

FROM A PSYCHIATRIST

I have been aware of Emotions Anonymous for many years and welcome the opportunity to endorse this very worthwhile self-help organization. It has come to my attention that there is a need for a book concerning Emotions Anonymous and that this would be very beneficial for countless thousands of people who do suffer from various types of emotional problems.

It is my opinion that Emotions Anonymous plays an important role in the overall treatment of people with emotional problems. The success of Alcoholics Anonymous could very easily be equaled by Emotions Anonymous as the years go on.

We at North Memorial Medical Center, Crisis Unit, had the distinct pleasure of helping to establish the Emotions Anonymous chapter at North Memorial Hospital. It has grown and is still an active chapter, meeting in the auditorium. I do refer many of my patients with emotional problems to your organization.

In summary, it is with great pleasure that I would like to recommend Emotions Anonymous to anyone with emotional problems. I believe that it is a very excellent self-help group and that it should become more successful through the years. I have no hesitations at all in referring my psychiatric patients there, and I do believe one of the big answers in the future to treatment of emotional problems will be through self-help groups like Emotions Anonymous.

James T. Garvey, M.D.
The Minneapolis Clinic of
Psychiatry and Neurology, LTD
Minneapolis, Minnesota

FROM A LAWYER

The daily requirements of life with its extreme pressure upon each individual, has often resulted in a breakdown of the fiber of happiness, stability, and self-esteem.

It has been my observation that an understanding and practice of the principles of Emotions Anonymous, as set forth in this book, has in many cases provided a vehicle by which the individual can accept, adjust and function fully, adequately, and comfortably in our modern society.

STANLEY J. MOSIO
Attorney At Law
St. Paul, Minnesota

CHAPTER IV

A DOCTOR'S OPINION

I am a doctor: medical doctor, neurologist, psychiatrist, psychotherapist, and specialist in psychosomatic medicine. As doctors, we were always trained to relieve pain, to cure diseases, to cure sickness, to cure mankind from dis-eases. It is so important to understand that any state or condition of dis-ease is not a sickness. The word "dis-ease" is a wonderful word when we see it in another context: separate the "dis" from the "ease" and it means a state in which you do not feel at ease anymore. We have the power through training to free people from everything that is bothering them, physically, mentally, or even spiritually.

These three parts are artificially divided but form a whole. In each cell of our body is the physical, the mental, and the spiritual part. You cannot separate them; they are a whole. The whole person cannot be separated into parts.

The separation was a result of the knowledge of the 18th century - that finally man who was always a whole became divided by scientists, into two parts - the mind and the body. In the 18th and 19th centuries special doctors became psychiatrists. The first known psychiatrist was Philippe Pinel, a Frenchman who was born in 1745 and died in Paris in 1826.

At this time, the division of body and mind created two different kinds of medicine - one for the body's physical condition and one for the mental condition.

We were trained, and this was my goal too, to relieve all pain, to make it disappear, so that we can really live our lives. This is the reason we developed many techniques to relieve pain and today we are in the century of the pain killers.

As a doctor it took me a long time to find that actually relieving pain is not my goal. I found that behind all the suffering, pain, diseases, and all the conditions that cause dis-ease, lie the thirst and the hunger of the human being for spirituality.

This hunger and thirst is the aspiration of a human being to be a whole again. Through the conquests of the brain, we are divided into three parts - spiritual, physical, and mental. We are running around as divided persons and we are lacking the knowledge of our origin, which is our Higher Power. We do not know where we have come from, where we are, or where we are going.

At any time that pain is present and we suffer, it shows us that we should do something about our spiritual needs. The pain shows us that our spiritual needs are not met. Doctors - medical doctors and mental doctors, psychiatrists, psychologists, psychotherapists, doctors dealing with both the physical and the mental side of the human being, specialists in psychosomatic medicine - have ignored this thirst and this hunger for being a whole, this hunger for spirituality. They were looking for techniques, for methods and theories with which they could give certain relief to suffering mankind, a relief from all pain.

They did not see that behind the pain was the hunger and thirst for spirituality. They did not say, "I understand your condition of feeling dis-ease in this world is an expression of hunger and thirst for spirituality." Instead, they invented methods to make people forget all this state of dis-ease.

They use methods where persons just do not feel anymore by putting them in a sleepy state. People become unaware of what they are really suffering from and actually craving for. They are put in a state where they are free from pain and free from feeling, called analgo-anaesthesy; it lets them forget about their real condition.

The industry created all the pain killers and so-called tranquillizers we have today; they created all the "wonderful" medications such as valium and librium which can be excellent when they are used at the right moment for a short time to relieve just enough pain so that the suffering human being may be able to open up and to accept the fact that behind his suffering is thirst and hunger.

We invented the electro-shock to make patients forget temporarily that there is a hunger and a thirst for closeness with other human beings, a closeness without fear or anger, and without being angry about themselves (because that is quite often the reason for suffering - that I cannot accept myself, my past, or my mistakes in life). Electro-shock makes one forget. We also invented a method called lobotomy.

Today we are using methods which shock only the non-dominant side of the brain - for someone who uses his right hand, the left side of the brain; and for someone who uses his left hand, the right side of the brain. The memory for emotions is located on the non-dominant side of the brain. Emotions express our divided self, the hunger and the thirst to feel at home in this world, to feel warmth, trust, and faith in our relationship to our origin. We can call it God.

You know many cannot call it God because they do not know anything about this relationship. You can only know something about your relationship with God if you experience it.

There are so many things said in Sunday School, in church, and in school about this spiritual relationship, but we cannot understand it if they are words which arrive only at a cerebral level. God can only be understood when God is experienced as in the Twelve-Step Program. That is what is happening in EA.

Actually medicine and medical doctors, psychiatrists, psychologists, and psychotherapists have unknowingly invented techniques to prove how we can live without pain by not acknowledging and by not being in contact with

God and our whole being. All the techniques are an attempt to live without stilling our hunger and thirst for closeness, warmth, intimacy, and a real, true relationship with God. Freud tried it. Jung tried it. Adler tried it. The Gestalt therapy, psychodrama, and all psychotherapy techniques try it. The hope that is created by using these techniques and the desire on the part of the patients to finally find relief and a solution to their problems hinder persons from doing it on their own - they are depending on the therapist and his techniques to do it for them.

When all these hopes created by psychotherapeutic techniques can be dropped and the persons hit bottom, a new relationship to themselves can be created, a new relationship to other human beings (this is what is happening in the Twelve-Step Program), and through all this, a new relationship to God.

I have not always been able to use the word "God." Someone told me that that is what would save my life but I ran like mad because I did not know what this person wanted to say. The mere telling of something, when it enters only through the ears and goes into the brain, does not create an understanding; it must be an experience. The price for this experience, as everyone tells in EA, is pain and suffering. One finally wakes up and finds there is nothing on earth (no doctor, no psychotherapist, no psychologist, no psychoanalyst, or no medication) that has the answer for this thirst. It is as if I could say to Richard, "I am thirsty. Would you go to the kitchen and drink for me?" This does not work. Maybe Richard would reply, "I am not thirsty, I do not want to drink." Even if he would do it for me, it would not help me; I have to go out to the kitchen or to the well and get the drink myself. No one can do it for me.

Medicine is hindering us. All the medication and all the techniques are, as it says in the New Testament - if someone is hungry and thirsty and you would give him, instead of bread, stones; instead of fish, snakes; and instead of water, maybe alcohol. (Alcohol does not still thirst either. Alcoholics know more about that.) Hunger and thirst are wonderful human needs which occur any time our needs are not met.

No human being is completely without hope when he feels hunger because we have finally learned to look for something which will still our hunger and our thirst. We know how to do it but we have never learned to still this emotional and spiritual thirst. Therefore, we feel horrible and we feel that it is a sickness. But depression is not a sickness; it is self-pity, frozen rage, a learned helplessness. Depression is only a defense mechanism to hide from conflict. Like the reflex an animal has to protect itself, a rabbit confronted by a snake freezes and this tells the snake, "I am no longer alive so there is no need to bite me." That is what we are doing in depression - we are hiding. We do not stay and face reality. All the other psychosomatic dis-eases are also states where we have not learned to meet our needs. These are alarm signals which tell us we should wake up and say, "Okay, do something about it."

Medicine is doing the opposite. Medicine is giving us something to help us forget our needs. Then we do not like ourselves, we cannot accept our past, and we experience the incapacity and the inadequacy to meet our own needs. We do so many real things that we are ashamed of, but these things, even crimes, are only the expression of our incapacity to meet our needs. We are even able to hurt somebody else because we cannot stand our own pain. We start hurting our neighbors and our environment.

What is happening in marriages, so often, is that we are miserable. Don't you feel miserable when you are hungry? If the nicest girl in the world came up to you and said, "I love you," you would ignore her and say, "I must have food to eat first." When you are really hungry, nothing can interest you except getting something to eat and drink. That is our condition when we have this spiritual hunger and this emotional hunger. We do weird things, even commit crimes. I believe crime is one of the issues. Crime is a result of needs not being met.

We are the result of our upbringing. I had the best parents in the world. Today I can say that, because I feel much better now at the age of fifty-four than I did many years ago. It took me fifty years to begin to feel at ease in this world. I always felt DIS-ease. Since I feel much better now and I know there is a purpose in life, I am able to say that my parents did the best they could. Therefore, I know that whatever my parents did or neglected to do does not matter. My parents did right. Even if they were alive today (which my mother is), they do not have to do anything more for me. I am NOW RESPONSIBLE (response-able).

Do you know how wonderful that word is? It is the same in English, French, and German. It means to become able to respond. Responsible means learning to respond with the right answer to life's challenges, evocations, and confrontations. This is fun; this is a pleasure for me. We should find the right answer with our partner. A partner is not only you, here and now, but also the way in which I decorate an apartment because that is a part of me. The weather, climate, wind, the country I was born in, the language I speak and the languages I learn to speak, the floor, the touching, the feeling of a tissue, all become my partners in "song and melody."

The way we respond is the dialogue we are engaged in. The very moment when the sperm and the egg unite, in that very moment, a dialogue starts. I had the pleasure of seeing under the microscope what happens when the sperm and the egg unite. The "dialogue" has begun. You cannot separate them anymore - they are talking and talking and talking.

After a while we see them talking, they are even sticking out. They are adding talks and talks and cells and cells to each other and the result that speaks is a newborn baby. You and I are the result of such dialogue. Is this not wonderful?

After nine months, we are literally thrown onto this earth - we are separated; the umbilical cord is cut. This new person's dialogue with the world is started.

Childbirth is violent. According to the new Lamaze method, the birth is carried out in silence, with dimmed lights, and warmth (it is as warm as in the uterus). There is no rush. The baby is not taken out like a rabbit and slapped on the backside to make him breathe. In this method, the mother assists the baby out of her womb after the head and shoulders are born, and places the baby on her naked belly and breasts. The umbilical cord is still uncut. The baby is given time to breathe. Its own circulatory system is given time to function. The cord is cut. Then the baby is given a bath to remove the protective coating and it is given time to experiment with its new freedom. Its dialogue starts then with the world, the climate, the language.

The baby already knows the voice of the mother and through the chemistry of the blood is in touch with the emotions of the mother. The baby knows the whole history of the marriage, the whole history of the mother. After the baby is born, we try to hide all this!

So the dialogue starts. The baby is not helpless. That's just the way we see it. It is a "baby" for many months and then it is an "infant" for many years. It grows up and has to learn again what was first learned as a fetus and as a baby, not to be afraid of its needs.

A baby is not afraid of expressing its needs. A baby has power. When it screams at night it can even wake up fathers! What power! The baby shows its needs, power-fully.

Later on in life, we learn we must meet our own needs and sometimes we must wait to have our needs fulfilled; we cannot always have instant gratification.

But we create, with our technology, an environment like a uterus, like a womb, in which we can get, as we experienced before birth and as an infant: instant pleasure, no responsibility, a maximum of safety and power. We get instant light by merely pushing a button. We adjust the thermostat and have instant warmth. We go into an elevator and have instant elevation. Everything is done for us. We create our womb all over again and then we wonder why we do not want to make any strenuous effort to meet our own needs. We assume that our needs will be met, by someone. Our society created by infants for infants gives birth to infantile monsters.

If one does not use or exercise his limbs and muscles, they become weaker and weaker. It is the same with our spiritual muscles, they become thinner and thinner. We are astounded when life offers us a challenge and we are not able to meet the challenge. We feel, quite naturally, DIS-use, result of an atrophy.

Our modern society provides people responsible for meeting our needs. We have thin spiritual muscles and we pay these people. They are our gigolos. They carry us around and say, "Oh, it is not that bad! I have the answer. Don't worry! You do not have to look for an answer because I have it. In our chemical "kitchen" we have made some stuff for you that will make everything okay. You will not feel the pain of your dis-ease anymore."

That is a crime. A child learns to get up from a lying-down position when it sees others standing up and walking. The child imitates. He raises his head, sits up, and this is wonderful. All are exercises to become a grown-up person, but society does everything after the child is grown to prevent him from standing up for something. Society prevents him from being responsible.

We have created many things in our modern society that take over our ability to respond. The best thing that can happen to a person in our society is to get sick (sick and tired of being sick and tired of his condition in this world) and to feel dis-ease, to feel this alarm signal that tells him his needs are not being met. The person can then start to do something about fulfilling those needs.

Solutions offered to us through medicine, psychology and psychotherapy do not meet our real needs. Sometimes medicine is wonderful because it enables us to survive a condition where we might die. Medicine and modern surgery can save your life, but doctors only help us survive so that we can find our own way to meet our needs. They are enablers.

Bill W. and Dr. Bob founded the Twelve-Step Program because medicine, psychiatry, psychology, psychotherapy, psychoanalysis, social work, and religion - all the helping professions - no longer had an answer for the suffering of human beings. No answer was the answer. Bill W. and Dr. Bob had to decide whether to die or to live. They decided to live.

It would have been a disaster if medicine or psychotherapy had interfered with the foundation of AA and the Twelve-Step Program. Each one of us has the answer within us but it is hidden by the outside things, our false beliefs, our false gods. When Bill W. reached the point where nothing was left - no concept of life, no theory, no religion - he had to find his answer, the answer he had inside himself. This was the creation of the Twelve-Step Program.

Everyone who can identify with another human being in a Twelve-Step Program can find his answer, can find his true self. The Twelve-Step Program is a program where you are led to the point of giving up all - absolutely all - previous false beliefs, theories, concepts, and all hopes that an outside means or an outside power such as an earthly or human power, can restore your sanity.

This means surrender (a word coined by Dr. Harry M. Tiebout who was one of the first psychoanalysts who became a friend of Alcoholics Anonymous). We are learning to do acts of surrender by attending EA meetings.

I am not capable of surrendering totally. I have to surrender in portions, many thousands of little portions. This is happening in meetings. By adding up all the many little acts of surrender, we can arrive eventually at a state of surrender. Every day we have to do our acts of surrender.

EA is a training program, a school, and a university of life, where we can discover our real needs. We can discover that our needs are not good or bad, they are normal, they are biological, they are not poison or a burden. Perhaps you have learned in your family that your needs are natural, that they are beautiful like a bouquet of flowers. Sharing our needs with each other, being close and open with each other, is beautiful.. It is the best thing that can happen on earth. We have to learn to trust somebody. If someone thanks you at our meetings, they are meaning, "Thank you for being open with me. You trusted me." We have to learn gratitude, to be thankful that this exists and might happen. I am very thankful that you have taken the time to read what I have to say - that we have had the opportunity to come together. This is a fulfillment that is extremely rewarding. I cannot imagine anything more rewarding right now than to share feelings with one another. This sharing can help us get through many things that are not solved yet.

We still have many conditions that remain as hunger and thirst but we know that it is possible to still this hunger and thirst. We are not alone anymore.

We can get help from listening to others but we learn to give more of the right answers by becoming responsible for ourselves. Gradually we must become a grown-up person who can really say, "I owe everything to others and no one owes me anything. My parents do not owe me anything, my mate does not owe me anything. I set them free!"

By setting them free, by forgiving them, WE become free. WE BECOME FREE. That is a wonderful feeling!

This also includes forgiving ourselves; if we cannot forgive ourselves, there is no way to forgive another and be forgiven by God.

Through all this new experience of feeling, I now know I have the right to exist. I am entitled to have my needs met and I am entitled to be on this earth. Everybody else around me gives me the right to live. I can share joy and pleasure with other human beings. Joy and pleasure are food for each of us. We are so rich in having all this fullness inside of us, which we can hand out to each other every time we meet.

By growing up in this way, we can find our true identity and sanity that no human method or technique ever will promise us.

Walther H. Lechler
Psychosomatische Klinik
Bad Herrenalb, Western Germany

CHAPTER V

THE ENORMITY OF EMOTIONAL ILLNESS

Emotional Illness
and
The Hope Emotions Anonymous Has To Offer

I believe
Emotional illness can cripple us mentally, physically, and spiritually.

Emotional illness is no respecter of intelligence, education, wealth, or social status.

It affects not only ourselves but those who live with us and love us. Emotional illness becomes a family illness.

I believe
When we are in the midst of emotional illness it is hard to realize its enormity. We can understand and assess its vastness only after we have seen the changes we and others have made with the help of the Emotions Anonymous Twelve-Step Program.

Let us look at ourselves and the help Emotions Anonymous has to offer.

Let us see what we can do today to move in the right direction toward emotional health and happiness.

THE ILLNESS

I believe it is sometimes hard for us to realize how healthy -- or sick -- we are. In our search for self-worth, for identity, we may have unknowingly set unrealistic ideals and goals for ourselves which we can never live up to, so that our sense of self-worth is low and our ideals too high. How can we help but fail?

I believe
> We want to have no conflict, but we still have conflict.
> We want life to be perfect here and now but it is far from perfect.
> We want to have constant pleasure but we have pain.
> We so want to succeed in every effort we make that when we fail in one area we reject not only our actions but ourselves as well.
> We become very fearful.
> We try to impress other people by being something we are not, by being phony.
> We find ourselves being resentful toward people and life.
> We become experts at manipulating people.
> We become very self-centered.

I believe many of these things happen gradually and we may not even be aware of their presence and influence in our lives.

I believe that emotional illness can be a progressive and chronic illness. If it is not faced and dealt with, we can end up in a mental institution, commit suicide, or suffer from a physical illness brought on by our emotions.

I believe that our physical well-being is affected by our thoughts, attitudes, and emotions. Some of us have tried to cop-out from getting help for our emotional problems by questioning — "Is this a physical illness? Is this a mental illness? Or is this a spiritual illness?"

Body, mind, and spirit make up our total human life. Each is an integral part of us and each is influenced by the others. We really cannot divide ourselves as human beings.

In the Emotions Anonymous Program
> We do not analyze emotional illness.
> We do not label and categorize everything.
> We stop using our feeling of "uniqueness" as an excuse.
> We stop comparing ourselves with others.
> We stop blaming ourselves and others.
> We stop feeling sorry for ourselves.
> We stop being defiant.
> We stop denying our illness.
> We stop making excuses.
> We stop trying to convince ourselves that we are "different" from others.

These kinds of behavior are cop-outs, and the only purpose they serve is to perpetuate our illness. We can get help here IF we really want to be well.

I believe
> The only person keeping us from becoming well is OURSELVES.
>
> It is our own responsibility, our response to our ability to be emotionally well and healthy.
>
> We can put our past behind us and start anew, living one day at a time.
>
> It takes conscious effort on our part.
>
> It may not be easy at first, but it is possible.

TODAY IS THE FIRST DAY OF THE
REST OF OUR LIVES!

THE NATURE OF THE HUMAN MIND

I believe that while we cannot fully understand the working of the human mind, we know it is influenced by everything we see, hear, smell, taste, and feel. Many of our everyday actions become habit. Automatic! We are grateful for this, or we would have to learn to read and write, learn to eat, and learn to do many other things again and again.

I believe we also develop habits of thought. The THOUGHT pattern we follow develops our attitudes toward life. These ATTITUDES make us well and happy or sick and miserable, depending on how we choose to think.

Here are some questions to ponder:

Is my cup half-full or half-empty?
Is a failure someone who does not succeed or someone who never tries?
Do I feel I can do something today to help myself?
Am I able to forgive and forget hurts?
Do I need other people?
If something is worth doing, is it worth doing poorly?
Am I able to see good in myself?
Is happiness a matter of chance?
Do I think turning to a Higher Power can help me?
Are my emotional (nervous) problems too unique to be helped?
Am I too old to change?
Who is responsible for my feelings?

What thought pattern do we follow? Do our answers to the foregoing questions leave the door open for growth? Do the answers allow us to develop our full potential? If so, I believe these indicate a positive outlook, and we can have feelings of self-worth, can be happy in spite of problems, have energy to meet our daily tasks, can adjust to life even if it doesn't come up to our expectations, and have peace of mind even when faced with difficulties. We can have purpose to our life; we can radiate warmth and love; we can be optimistic and able to accept ourselves and others; we feel useful and as if we belong.

If, on the other hand, our answers indicate a rejection of self and criticism of others, a feeling of hopelessness, or a defeatist attitude, then I believe they reflect negative thinking on our part. We may have one or more symptoms, such as anxiety, panic, abnormal fears, guilt, depression, self-pity, remorse, worry, insomnia, tension, loneliness, withdrawal, boredom, fatigue, despair. We may experience compulsive behavior, obsessive thoughts, scrupulosity, suicidal and possibly homicidal tendencies, psychosomatic and physical illnesses.

If we are now experiencing any of these symptoms, we must change our thought pattern or we will stay sick.

In the ordinary course of a day many, many thoughts pass through our minds. Some of them may be negative. I believe it is not the occasional negative thought that causes trouble but our dwelling on it, denying it, or feeling guilty about it.

I believe that when we first developed these negative attitudes we did so to protect ourselves from the pain of rejection by others and ourselves. Self-preservation can take many forms.

I believe we chose our behavior and attitudes to escape from reality and from the responsibility for ourselves and our actions. For a time these attitudes seemed to help us, but as we built negative thought after negative thought we became engulfed in such painful symptoms we did not know where to turn.

Some of us sought help, but we could not accept the help offered. We may have sought independence and hated ourselves for the dependence we felt. I believe what we needed was interdependence with people, involving sharing-type relationships. We either put ourselves below everybody (feeling inferior) or above everybody (feeling superior), instead of recognizing the common humanity we all share.

I believe our symptoms allowed us to avoid the reality of today — the reality we couldn't seem to face. Little did we realize that reality is heaven compared to the hell we live in with our symptoms.

AWARENESS

I believe we finally come to a realization of our true state of emotional health and say to ourselves, "I have to get well. I can't stand living like this any longer. If I don't get well, I'm going to lose everything — my family, my friends, my job, my peace of mind. I'm hurting myself and everyone with whom I come in contact."

Intellectually we may understand this dilemma but I believe that in our illness we had built up such a pattern of negative thoughts and attitudes toward life that change cannot come overnight. Responding inadequately has been a habit too long. Our intellect says, "I want to get well and stay well." Our emotions say, "I don't want to let go of my old attitudes and behavior. These are all that I know, and I am afraid of change, afraid of the unknown."

Left to ourselves, we may be helpless — helpless but not hopeless. I believe that what we had really feared was ourselves — not only our imperfections but our abilities as well. Before we can be well we have to realize we are not meant to be perfect, for only God is Perfect. We are meant to be 'perfectly human' and that means to be just ourselves.

Granted, we become aware of many faults in ourselves, but we also discover many good qualities we never knew we had.

Being ourselves is not unchanging. We are always in the process of growth, of discovering a little more of ourselves. There is joy and satisfaction in this discovery.

I believe having emotional problems should carry no more guilt than having cancer or heart disease. I believe the guilt comes when we know we are sick and CAN get help but reject the help offered.

The question then is...Do I want to get well more than I want to stay sick?

Here is the decision no one can make for another.

What can we do about this illness, the enormity of it? UNTIL WE ACCEPT THE FACT OF OUR ILLNESS, WE WILL NOT DO THOSE THINGS WE NEED TO DO IN ORDER TO GET WELL.

MOVING IN THE RIGHT DIRECTION

The Twelve-Step Program of Emotions Anonymous is the answer to our problems. Emotions Anonymous (EA) is based on the same time-proven program of Alcoholics Anonymous. The first step in getting help from the Twelve Steps is to admit we are powerless over our emotions, that our lives have become unmanageable. We admit this not only on an intellectual level but accept it on an emotional (gut) level as well. This first step may not be easy.

This means we admit we are powerless over our emotions, that our lives are unmanageable, that we are not self-sufficient. Are we "too big and powerful" by ourselves to make such an admission? If we want to be well, I believe we must come to believe in some Power in the universe greater than we are. We must BECOME WILLING to turn our will and lives over to the care of "God" as we understand Him. This surrender is only possible IF we want to get well.   For fight as we might, this is the only place where surrender really brings true victory.

The Emotions Anonymous Program is a living program. We don't just join it. WE TRY TO LIVE IT, all Twelve Steps. We find it works. I believe it can work for anybody.

It is a program of honesty, honesty to ourselves. I believe we can learn to live at peace with unsolved problems — that is what serenity is. Do we really want to be well? As we apply this program, I believe we find we become more free, free at last to be ourselves. IF we want to be well, WE WILL pick up the Twelve Steps and use them. It is a chance to learn how to live. I believe if we stay sick we have no one to blame but ourselves.

With patience on our part, we can become happier than we ever dreamed was possible. The more we are able to share our strengths, hopes and imperfections, the more we grow. We find we really keep only what we are willing to give away.

The Third Step says we "Made a decision to turn our will and our lives over to the care of God *as we understood Him.*" I believe decision is the big word here. Make a commitment — to a Higher Power and to this Program! We can make it only by working the Program for ourselves. No one can do it for us. We have to let go of the old ways of self-reliance and self-sufficiency.

I believe we find hope as we come to EA and meet other people who have found help by learning to live this way of life. A chance to be well is something some of us did not know was possible. As we attend our weekly meetings we no longer feel alone. At last we feel we belong somewhere.

The love and acceptance we experience in the group help us accept ourselves. When others accept us as we are, it helps us to accept ourselves as we are. Only then are we free to change.

Acceptance does not necessarily mean we will like what we are. Acceptance does not mean we will stay as we are.

Acceptance means admitting what we are at this moment and realizing we are powerless to change by our own will power. Acceptance is being real about ourselves — saying what we really feel instead of what we think we should feel or what society might say we should feel. When others accept our feelings without trying to analyze them or judge them we find the courage to be more honest with ourselves. In this atmosphere we do indeed grow.

As we grow, I believe we experience the pain of healing, since there is pain connected with the recovery of every illness, both physical and emotional.

I believe this healing pain is a sign of our opening up to life and self, a feeling of newness, of discovery. But greater than the pain is the reward of an enriching life. Heal and grow we must. If we don't we will surely die — at least inside. As we grow, I believe we become more the unique person we are capable of being.

WITH the help of the Twelve Steps . . .

We find a new way of life.

WITH the acceptance and encouragement from the friends we make in the Program . . .

We learn to love and accept ourselves and others.

WITH the help of a Higher Power . . .

We find
The SERENITY to accept the things

we cannot change.

The COURAGE to change the things
we can, and

The WISDOM to know the difference.

WITH the help of all three . . .

We find ourselves
And the reason for our existence.

WE HAVE A CHOICE

A few words of encouragement to the person who has read this chapter. At one time or other I have experienced the hell of every symptom listed within.

I felt hopeless and helpless — in EA I have found a purpose for my existence. I have changed from feeling useless to feeling useful. I know in my heart this Program has saved my life.

I wish to express my gratitude to God as I understand Him' for the gift of the Twelve-Step Program of Emotions Anonymous.

I wish also to express my love and appreciation to those persons who encouraged me and shared themselves and their experiences with me.

An EA Member

MY CHART OF EMOTIONAL

This chart shows the progression of steps that many of us went through when we found health through the Twelve-Step Program of Emotions Anonymous. Each one's emotional bottom may come at a different depth.

I have minor difficulties
I have increasing problems
I have disagreements with family and friends
I have the blues
I have irritable reactions
I am worried and anxious
I have feelings of guilt
I indulge in daydreaming
I have psychosomatic ailments
I feel depressed
I feel indifferent to duty and self
I am losing interest in usual activities
I make excuses
I have a tendency toward use of prescribed drugs
I try a change of location
I blame other people and/or causes
I withdraw and avoid other people
I feel inferior
My depression becomes chronic
I become dependent upon prescribed or other drugs
I am unable to function
My loneliness becomes severe
I am preoccupied with myself and my problems
I am unable to concentrate
I make varied and frustrating attempts to get help
I am afraid of living and of dying
I have an irrational but overwhelming fear
I feel panic and terror
I abuse drugs
My alibi system collapses
I feel I am a failure
I consider suicide
I am in complete despair

EMOTIONAL BOTTOM

ILLNESS & RECOVERY

We can start upward toward recovery from our own emotional bottom when we truly accept the help of the EA Twelve-Step Program.

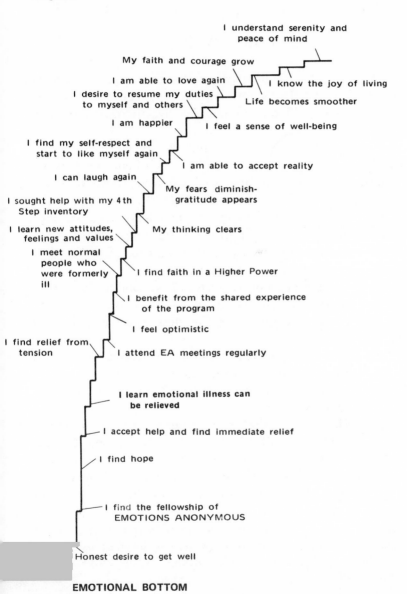

I understand serenity and peace of mind

My faith and courage grow

I am able to love again

I know the joy of living

I desire to resume my duties to myself and others

Life becomes smoother

I am happier

I feel a sense of well-being

I find my self-respect and start to like myself again

I am able to accept reality

I can laugh again

My fears diminish-gratitude appears

I sought help with my 4th Step inventory

I learn new attitudes, feelings and values

My thinking clears

I meet normal people who were formerly ill

I find faith in a Higher Power

I benefit from the shared experience of the program

I feel optimistic

I find relief from tension

I attend EA meetings regularly

I learn emotional illness can be relieved

I accept help and find immediate relief

I find hope

I find the fellowship of EMOTIONS ANONYMOUS

Honest desire to get well

EMOTIONAL BOTTOM

CHAPTER VI

HOW IT WORKS

Anyone who has diligently followed our path has never been known to fail. "Those who do not recover are people who cannot or will not completely give themselves to this simple program."*

If you are hurting and would like to change, you are probably willing to try anything that will help. Our stories tell how we once were, how we used the Twelve-Step Program, and what we are like now. These Twelve Steps are:

1. We admitted we were powerless over our emotions — that our lives had become unmanageable.
2. Came to believe that a Power greater than ourselves could restore us to sanity.
3. Made a decision to turn our will and our lives over to the care of God *as we understood Him.*
4. Made a searching and fearless moral inventory of ourselves.
5. Admitted to God, to ourselves, and to another human being the exact nature of our wrongs.
6. Were entirely ready to have God remove all these defects of character.
7. Humbly asked Him to remove our shortcomings.
8. Made a list of all persons we had harmed, and became willing to make amends to them all.
9. Made direct amends to such people wherever possible, except when to do so would injure them or others.

*From Page 58, *ALCOHOLICS ANONYMOUS*, copyright 1939, by Alcoholics Anonymous World Services, Inc. Reprinted by permission of Alcoholics Anonymous World Services, Inc.

10. Continued to take personal inventory and when we were wrong promptly admitted it.

11. Sought through prayer and meditation to improve our conscious contact with God *as we understood Him,* praying only for knowledge of His will for us and the power to carry that out.

12. Having had a spiritual awakening as the result of these Steps, we tried to carry this message, and to practice these principles in all our affairs.

Some of the Steps seemed difficult. We thought there must be an easier way but there was not. From the very beginning we urge you to be "fearless" and thorough in following these Steps. Some of us tried to hold onto our old ways but found we could not grow in the Program until we let go entirely.

We discovered through the Program that God, *as we understood Him,* helped us to comprehend and begin working these Steps as completely as we could, to the best of our ability. Through daily practice of these Steps we discovered ourselves. We grew emotionally and spiritually.

STEP ONE

We admitted we were powerless over our emotions - that our lives had become unmanageable.

POWERLESS

When we first went to an Emotions Anonymous meeting and heard people say they were "powerless," many of us rebelled for we certainly were not powerless. Even after several meetings we were still puzzled by the word. Perhaps you, too, are uncertain as to whether you are really powerless over your emotions. Look at some of these descriptions of how powerlessness affected some of us and see if any apply to you:

- We were unable to start or stop an emotion.
- We were helpless, however, not hopeless.
- We could not get well by ourselves; we needed help.

- We tried analyzing, but it didn't work.
- We were not able to change by using our own will power.
- We were not self-sufficient; we needed other people.
- We were powerless over our feelings, positive or negative.

Did you ever become angry with someone and try to make that anger go away by using logic and reason? Did you ever feel guilty about something and try to rationalize it away? Did you ever say or think, "Why does everything have to happen to me?" Then, we believe, you are powerless over your emotions!

When we finally come to realize we are powerless, we usually back off and look for a new direction.

UNMANAGEABLE

Is your life truly unmanageable? Ask yourself if any or all of these statements apply to you:

- The more we want to control our behavior, the more out of control we become.
- We would like to think that our lives are not unmanageable, that it is those around us who make it so. We must realize that we are powerless over other people. The only person we can change is ourself. We cannot change another person.
- We are over-sensitive (touchy) to what others say. In our self-centeredness we take the everyday occurrences and actions of other people too personally and too seriously.
- We don't talk to others because they "wouldn't want to talk to us."
- We feel different and alone.

So often we feel there has to be a reason for what happens. The direction our life has taken may be due to loneliness, insecurity, shyness, not feeling okay about self, fear of rejection, fear of failure, fear of not belonging, fear of being different, feelings of inadequacy, rejection of self, being overly concerned with self, self-denial, or fear of involvement. Some of the symptoms that may arise out of these causes include various psychosomatic illnesses such as ulcers, stomach pains, headache, hypertension, skin disorders, non-organic digestive and intestinal disorders and complaints, non-organic heart and circulatory irregularities, urinary, back, muscle and joint complaints. Of course, all physical complaints should be checked out medically, but once we become aware that there is no organic reason for these problems, we must suspect an emotional basis and start looking for the answers.

We may suffer from compulsive perfectionism. If we cannot do something perfect, we consider ourselves a failure. Or we may sit back and be an "acceptor" -- whatever others do or say, our only role is to accept. We may not be happy in this role and probably begin to storm inside but we are not capable of asserting ourselves in various situations (this often leads to aggression in other areas where we feel more in control. For example, persons who have difficulty with their employers and/or co-workers come home and take out their frustrations on their families). Contrarily, we may be a "rejector." Nothing anyone else does or says is acceptable to us. One can well imagine what kind of relationships rejectors have with those around them and what kind of emotional upheavals occur in the lives of such persons.

We may be accident prone or suffer from depression or anxiety. We may be very nervous and panicky. We may have suicidal or homicidal tendencies, not be able to sleep. We probably worry a great deal, withdraw from others, become irritable, perhaps even abuse those we love. We may even feel others are talking about us, watching our every move, or are out to get us. Abnormal rage and temper tantrums are often symptoms that make us realize something is very wrong. We come to realize that intellect and emotions are separate. Adding two and two is using intellect; anger is using an emotion. We are often apathetic, judgmental. We

procrastinate and are phony. We criticize others for it seems
to make us feel better about ourselves, but we may also tend
to let others walk all over us. We have feelings of self-pity,
resentment, anger, jealousy, envy, greed, intolerance, im-
patience, lust, selfishness, oversensitivity, vanity, indif-
ference, or any of the many character defects that are a
part of one whose life has become unmanageable.

We may try various ways to escape from these feelings.
Some of us used our intellect to rationalize our feelings away.
Some of the more common escapes are pills, alcohol, food,
sleep, or work. Even talking, silence, reading, travel, or going
to school may become an escape when used to excess. We,
ourselves, have been or know someone who is a compulsive
talker or a television addict who lets the rest of the world
go by while lying on the couch with eyes glued to the TV.

When our particular escape does not work, we look
elsewhere for the help we so desperately need. In turning
to EA and the Twelve Steps as a possible answer, we are
admitting we have hit our emotional bottom. For some that
means hospitalization or visits to a psychiatrist, but not all.
That emotional bottom is different for each person. Some
come into Emotions Anonymous in an effort to help another
person but once there, realize they also need help. One
thing we all have in common is that our bottom is where we
decide we want to do something today to change our lives.
We are sick and tired of our old way of life. We may even
reach the depths of despair. Wherever our bottom is, we are
tired of being the way we are.

ADMITTING

Admitting we cannot manage our lives is not easy. It
is not easy to admit our self-centeredness, to stop blaming
others for the way we are, the way we behave. We say, "If
my spouse were different," or "If it weren't for my children,
my mother or father, my boss, my job, my in-laws, the
climate, my home, my car - anything or anybody - I wouldn't
be like this."

Through Step One we begin to learn to accept our emotions as they are and not allow them to control our behavior. As we learn to accept our emotions, we are better able to manage our lives rather than having our lives manage us.

Admitting our defects is an act of humility and also of honesty. We may have been powerless all of our lives, but only now do we recognize and admit it. When we admit we are powerless over our emotions we recognize the fact that we have no will in the matter. The strength to maintain our health must come from the outside, from our Higher Power, and this we shall consider in Step Two.

Some think of the First Step as despair, but for us it is a Step of hope because we find we are not alone. There is help. In Step Two our hope grows.

STEP TWO

Came to believe that a Power greater than ourselves could restore us to sanity.

Some of us had no concept of a Higher Power. Some viewed our Higher Power only as something to be feared and someone capable of punishment. Others believed they had a good relationship with their Higher Power. Still others, through their intellect, had decided there was no God. Some of us were searching for a Higher Power. In Step Two we came to realize the importance of believing in a power greater than ourselves. This could be the traditional God, the group (the group is greater than I am), nature (a force that is certainly greater than I), or anything we can accept as being greater than ourselves.

CAME TO BELIEVE

First we came to a meeting. Some of us became aware that we did not have any self-worth, that we did not feel worthy for a Higher Power to help us. Then we came to realize that we are equal to all others in God's eyes, and He would help us. Then we came to believe a Higher Power could restore us to sanity, given a willingness and an open-mindedness on our part.

Many of us had our day of defying God, perhaps because God had not delivered what we had asked for - as a greedy child making an impossible list for Santa Claus. Perhaps we had met with some great sorrow or disappointment and thought God had deserted us. We may have experienced illness and asked God to make us well, but nothing happened.

EA revealed to us how destructive our defiance was. "At no time had we asked what was God's will for us; instead we had been telling Him what it *ought* to be. No person can believe in God and defy Him too. Belief meant reliance, not defiance."*

Coming into the Program, some of us thought we were full of faith. We prayed, attended church faithfully, and did what we thought were the right things. We found the answer to our problem was in the quality of our faith, not the quantity. We thought we had humility but did not.

Others of us looked with envy at those who believed. Weren't they lucky? Perhaps by coming to the meetings we would come to believe, too. But, of course, we learned that believing does not just happen. We must work at it. With belief comes faith, a willingness to trust in the unknown, to trust in a Higher Power to restore us to that sanity we so desperately want.

Believing in a Power greater than ourselves is different from having faith in a Higher Power. We cannot claim faith if we talk about our fears and anxieties at the same time. Faith comes as we see God work in our lives or in the lives of others. Our lives may improve without believing in God, but we cannot reach the ultimate serenity without true belief in a Higher Power.

Many have found, through working the Twelve Steps, that their concept of a Higher Power develops into a deep personal relationship with God, one that had not been possible before the Program.

*From Page 32, *TWELVE STEPS AND TWELVE TRADITIONS*, copyright 1952, by Alcoholics Anonymous World Services, Inc. Reprinted by permission of Alcoholics Anonymous World Services, Inc.

POWER GREATER THAN OURSELVES

No longer able to manage our lives, to live at peace with ourselves and others, we have been forced to turn to a Higher Power out of desperation. Everything depends upon faith in a Higher Power - our future in EA, serenity, happiness, and well-being. Faith is commitment and belief in a power greater than ourselves. Our Higher Power finds us right where we are; we do not have to find Him. If we have difficulty finding our Higher Power, we can begin by trusting another human being. In Step Two it is necessary that we admit the existence of a Higher Power. Once we realize that we are not all-powerful, we can stop playing God and let God be God.

SANITY

Sanity is sane thinking, common sense. The dictionary defines sanity as reasonable behavior, and most of us know our behavior was anything but reasonable. The word sanity in Step Two was difficult to accept for some of us. However, we need only to look at our behavior in the past - temper tantrums, uncontrolled anger, silence, excessive sleep, or excessive anything - to know our behavior was certainly not sane or rational. After giving the matter some thought we had to admit the word sanity was appropriate. The more fully we admit that only God can restore us to sanity, the more we will seek His help as the solution to our problems and difficulties and the more willing we will be to make our Third Step decision, to turn our will and lives over to Him.

STEP THREE

Made a decision to turn our will and our lives over to the care of God as we understood Him.

In Step Three we come face to face with our dilemma. The more we deny or fight our feelings, the more the depression, anxieties, and fears close in. Once we acknowledge our weaknesses, we can start to built a new life. We must stop trying to be self-sufficient if we want to get well. Let's face it - on our own we messed things up. The first three Steps are pivotal. We must come back to them time and time again. Since emotions are not a tangible thing, we must admit that we cannot change ourselves by will power alone.

Acceptance of ourselves, of others, of our situations is the basis of the first three Steps. Acceptance is not apathy. Acceptance is: "This is I; this is the best I can do today. Stop fighting." Apathy says, "I give up. It isn't worth it. I don't care." Acceptance frees us to change. Apathy keeps us locked into our illness.

MADE A DECISION

We were fearful of making a commitment. After being in the Program for some time, we realized we had to make a decision. When we first made the decision to turn our lives over to a Higher Power we felt good about it, but perhaps were very frightened about carrying it out. When we surrendered ourselves as we were - symptoms, feelings, and all - only then could a Higher Power help us.

OUR WILL AND OUR LIVES

Through the Program we learned that we could not live successfully on self-will alone. We were so often in collision with something or somebody even though our motives were good. Most people try to live by self-will, like an actor who wants to run the whole show, forever trying to arrange the lights, the ballet, the scenery, and the rest of the players in his own way. If his arrangements would only stay put, if people would just do as he wished, the show would be great. Everyone, including himself, would be pleased. Life would be wonderful. In trying to make these arrangements our actor may sometimes be quite virtuous. He may be kind, considerate, patient, generous, even modest and self-sacrificing. On the other hand, he may be mean, egotistical, selfish, and dishonest. As with most humans, he is more likely to be a composite of these. Most of us are concerned with ourselves, whatever our motives.

Driven by fears of all kinds, self-delusion, and self-pity,

we step on the toes of others and they retaliate. Sometimes they hurt us. Our words and actions often place us in a position that allows us to be hurt. So basically, our troubles are of our own making. They arise out of ourselves, a result of self-will run rampant, though we usually don't recognize the problem. It is essential we rid ourselves of this selfishness. We were unable to reduce our self-centeredness by wishing it away or using our own power. We had to have God's help. Until we learned to trust people we could not trust God. Until we could start trusting Him we could not turn our will over to Him. We cannot analyze God's will. We do not always know God's will for us. When we begin to know ourselves we can begin to recognize His direction for us.

Before we could turn our will over to a Higher Power we had to accept defeat. Making this decision was a commitment to use the Program. This commitment is a form of love. We must be willing to try. We cannot fold our hands and say, "God, do everything." We are the ones who have to take action.

THE CARE OF GOD

When we let go, many remarkable things followed. Being all powerful, He provided what we needed as we let go. On such a footing we became less and less interested in ourselves, our little plans and designs. More and more we became interested in seeing what we could contribute to life around us. As we felt new power flow in, we began to enjoy peace of mind; as we discovered we could again face life, we became conscious of His presence - we began to lose our fear of yesterday, today, or tomorrow. We began to live one day at a time! As we turned to God out of desperation, we were freely given that which we, on our own, had been unable to find. When we decided to turn our will and our lives over to the care of God, we were freed from the agony of trying to be God ourselves, and released to Him the responsibility of managing our lives and the lives of those around us.

AS WE UNDERSTOOD HIM

. Since childhood many of us believed in a God of fear and punishment; for God to accept us, we thought we must obey and strive for perfection. Since He was watching us, keeping a score card on our wrongdoings, we would surely never measure up when the final tally was taken; we would be doomed. With that concept of God, it was very difficult to look at this Step and turn our lives over to the God of our childhood. We now wanted a God who would restore us to sanity, a power greater than ourselves, not a figment of our imagination or a product of our own will. If we had no conception of God, we asked that He give it to us. To want a God to suit our own tortured self is a contradiction of our admission that we are powerless. The sure way is to humbly pray, "God, I offer myself to Thee - to build with me and to do with me as Thou wilt. Relieve me of the bondage of self, that I may better do Thy will. Take away my difficulties that victory over them may bear witness to those I would help of Thy power, Thy love, and Thy way of life. May I do Thy will always!"*

We found a loving God!

We gave much thought to this Step, making sure we were ready. At last we could abandon ourselves entirely to Him. Now we were ready for the vigorous action of Step Four.

STEP FOUR

Made a searching and fearless moral inventory of ourselves.

We started a personal inventory. This was a non-judgmental approach to looking at ourselves and it was a frightening experience but a very necessary one. In a business, inventory includes all merchandise on hand. In doing our per-

*From Page 63, *ALCOHOLICS ANONYMOUS*, copyright 1939, by Alcoholics Anonymous World Services, Inc. Reprinted by permission of Alcoholics Anonymous World Services, Inc.

sonal inventory we wrote down every character trait, both positive and negative, and listed experiences from the past that bothered us. First we searched out the flaws which caused us to feel we had failed in life. We had to look within.

It was important to write down this inventory so that we would not forget anything when taking our Fifth Step. We could deal with it more objectively when we saw it in writing because it was less easy to rationalize.

SEARCHING

We searched thoroughly and honestly, covering all aspects of our personality. We did not exclude anything. Self-honesty brings self-acceptance. We have no defect that is unique; we are all human. Anything we allow ourselves to become aware of can be worked out. It may appear that our feelings are defects of character, but they are not. Feelings are neither good nor bad.

FEARLESS

Fearless does not mean painless. Fearless means that we may be frightened but we go ahead and take our inventory, nevertheless. Fearlessness is openness and honesty in looking within. The more unrealistic self-image we have, the more painful it is to uncover our defects. There is pain in every healing process but as we grow and face our pain in Step Four, it opens the way to the serenity we are searching for.

MORAL INVENTORY

Many times when we look at the word moral, we think of it as having something to do with sex, stealing, or lying. It is much more than that. Our prejudices, intolerance, criticisms, fears, and our guilts are all a part of our morality, as are selfishness, egotism, and resentment. Morality should come from within. It comes from beliefs and attitudes which we have accepted as truths from our childhood. In growing up we may have acquired guilt, shame, or embarrassment for our sexual thoughts, feelings, and experiences, and we need to bring these tormenting ghosts out into the open. We must stop judging others or ourselves. Hiding guilt and shame will keep us from becoming well. We will continue to reject ourselves and others until we deal with our humanness. Anger, self-pity, and resentment, when recognized, can be worked through without becoming a continual attitude or behavior problem. These attitudes or behaviors create our defects of character. For instance, to deny self-pity is to encourage an attitude of "Poor me, I've got it so tough." Understanding this, I can realize, first, I am human; second, I am not bad because I feel this way; and third, I can accept that this is part of me for the present. A defect of character will become less of a problem as soon as I am willing to work on it in Steps Five, Six, and Seven.

In starting our inventory, we usually deal with our resentments first (reliving hurts and pain). This feeling of ill toward another destroys more of us than anything else. When we resent someone, we unknowingly allow that person to control us. It hurts us but it may not hurt the person we resent. Harboring deep resentment leads only to a life of frustration and unhappiness.

In dealing with resentments, we put them on paper listing people, institutions, or principles with whom or which we are angry. We ask ourselves why we are angry. In most cases it is our self-esteem, our wallets, our ambitions, our personal relationships (including sex) that are hurt or threatened. We are frustrated. In taking our inventory, we list situations similar to the following examples. Was it our self-esteem, our security, our pride and ambition, our personal, or sex relationships which had been interfered with?

EXAMPLES

I'm Resentful at:	The Situation:	Affects My:
My friend	Ignored me and sometimes excluded me. Why should he/she do that to me?	Self-esteem, security, pride (Fear).

A person dealing with the public	Was indifferent, rude, didn't want to help me. "When I'm working, I don't treat people that way!"	Self-esteem, security, pride (Fear).
My employer	Unfair, unreasonable, promoted someone else to the position I was in line for, shows favoritism.	Self-esteem, pride, financial security (Fear).
Jane or John Doe	Pays too much attention to my spouse.	Sex relations, self-esteem (Fear).
Spouse	Hostile, criticizes, nags me or ignores me, doesn't understand, wants me to be more responsible. Wants me to be responsible for his/her happiness.	Pride, sex relations, security, self-esteem, (Fear).
Family	Does not appreciate me; they interfere. Not dependable; do not do what I want; do not take responsibility. Children will not ever grow up to be responsible adults.	Self-esteem, pride (Fear).

Looking at the inventory, we see the word "fear" in every example. In any of the above situations, the first emotion to take over is fear. Fear is the result of threats to our self-esteem, pride, and well being.

Next we list our abnormal or irrational fears. We review our past conduct - where had we been selfish, dishonest, or inconsiderate? Whom had we hurt? Did we have feelings of guilt? Did we unjustifiably arouse jealousy, suspicion, or bitterness?

In writing our inventory we concentrate only on our mistakes. In doing so we become aware of how really self-centered we are. Where had we been selfish, dishonest, self-seeking, and frightened? Though a situation may not have been entirely our fault, we consider only our own involvement. It is our inventory, not another person's. We see our faults and list them on paper. We admit our wrongs and are willing to set these matters straight.

If we were thorough about our personal inventory, we wrote down a lot. We dealt with our resentments and began to see their terrible destructiveness. We listed people we had hurt by our behavior and were able to use this list in our Eighth Step. We begin to learn tolerance and patience.

Through an honest personal inventory of ourselves, we became more aware of our humanness. We sought out the personality defects that made us uncomfortable, that caused us difficulty with ourselves and others. We also looked for our assets because our goal is to build a healthy, realistic image of what we are. We listed our good qualities and were surprised how many there were.

With this tangible evidence of our willingness to look at ourselves honestly, we are then ready to move forward to Step Five.

STEP FIVE

Admitted to God, to ourselves, and to another human being the exact nature of our wrongs.

All of EA's Twelve Steps ask us to go contrary to our natural desires; they all deflate our egos. But Step Five is absolutely necessary to an enduring serenity and peace of mind. If we have been honest in our Fourth Step, we may have certain distressing and humiliating memories that we hope will remain our secret because we are certain no one will ever understand or accept them. We may feel very lonely, isolated, and unique, but we must deal with the exact nature of our wrongs. It is necessary that we talk about the specific examples written down in Step Four; it is not enough to say that we are resentful, that we feel guilt.

We will not progress until we share this honest inventory with someone else. When we feel we are forgiven, we can more easily forgive others. Being alone with God may not seem as embarrassing as facing up to another person. God knows everything we have done and yet understands and still loves us. In dealing with our inventory, however, we must admit to God, to ourselves, and to another human being. Admitting may be compared to a three-legged stool. Without any one leg, it cannot stand. If we leave out God, ourselves, or another human being, our Fifth Step will not stand.

We have already admitted our wrongs somewhat by taking our inventory. We cannot wish or will our defects away. Too much guilt may cause us to exaggerate our shortcomings; on the other hand, anxiety or pride might be a smokescreen for hiding our defects. Solitary self-appraisal is not enough. We are under constant fear and tension which makes us want to escape from reality. Sharing with another person is the only way we can get a true picture of ourselves.

The Fifth Step is best taken with a person having a working knowledge of the Twelve-Step Program. It is very important that this person understand what we are trying to accomplish. He or she might be a clergyman, a doctor, a counselor or a similar receptive professional person. In the event a Fifth Step person is not available, we may choose a member who has been in the Program for a long time whom we consider trustworthy and understanding, who will not betray our confidence, and with whom we feel comfortable. A Fifth Step person may give insight, encouragement, or suggestions, but primarily he/she is a listener. Most of all this person will be accepting and non-judgmental. We go over everything in our inventory. If we knowingly omit something, we more than likely will continue to hang onto our misery. If we are determined to get well, we will be honest. Here is where the Program really requires courage. There is nothing a Fifth Step person has not heard before. By holding back nothing, we are on the road to recovery. Being honest with another person confirms that we are being honest with ourselves and with God.

What have we gained after completing Step Five? Very likely we have rid ourselves of the terrible sense of isolation and loneliness. We gained the feeling of belonging. We developed a kinship with man and God. Sometimes there is an immediate feeling of relief, and, as the pain subsides, a healing tranquility takes place. With some the relief comes more gradually and there is not this sudden feeling of release. Some of us may feel as if we're walking on "Cloud Nine." To some of us comes the realization that God really must love us to have sent this understanding, accepting Fifth Step person into our lives. Many of us who have taken this Fifth Step have actually felt the presence of God for the first time. Even those who thought they already had faith became conscious of God as never before. The terrible burden of guilt is lifted and a pervading sense of peace with man and God takes over.

Immediately following the Fifth Step, it is well to find a quiet place and carefully review what transpired, thanking God for allowing us to know Him better.

Now that we have gained some self-awareness and have shared this awareness, we are ready for the remaining Steps of the Program.

STEP SIX

Were entirely ready to have God remove all these defects of character.

In Step Four we made an inventory and listed our defects of character. In Step Five we shared what we had found with God and another human being. Now, in Step Six we strive to have these defects removed. That sounds so simple, for wouldn't anyone be ready to get rid of things that he knows have caused him to be ill? However, the nature of our illness is such that this is not as easy as it may seem. We are so comfortable with some of our defects that we do not like to even think about getting rid of them; they have been a part of our life for such a long time that we depend on them. We can only pray for the willingness to have the defects removed and realize that we cannot give all of them up at once. We must, however, never look at any of our defects and say, "This I will never give up."

We must accept the fact that we probably will never achieve perfection in practicing this Step. In accepting this, we are becoming ready to give up one of our biggest character defects, the need to be perfect. We must be patient and recognize that this is a lifetime job. We can prepare to have a few defects removed at a time. We must make a beginning, perhaps picking out the defect that causes us the most pain.

This is putting to use what we have learned in the Program - to be willing to change. The key word is "willingness." Until we make some attempt to be ready to have our defects removed, there is no way they will disappear by themselves.

Most of us wanted to be well yesterday but we did not get sick overnight and we cannot expect to get well in a short time. Even our readiness will not guarantee the removal of our defects; we must go on to Step Seven and humbly ask God to remove them.

STEP SEVEN

Humbly asked Him to remove our shortcomings.

In Step Six we take action in becoming ready to have God (as we understand Him) remove our defects of character. In Step Seven we ask God to remove them. The efforts are ours; the results are God's.

When we become aware of our defects, we will not succeed in removing them until we ask for God's help. Defects are often the result of defenses built up to protect ourselves from hurt, and it may take many years to remove some of them.

Humility is the key word to working Step Seven. When we first came into the Program humility had different meanings for most of us. Some thought humility meant walking around with stooped shoulders, feeling we were inferior to other people. If we felt self-confident or saw good in ourselves, we might feel, or others might tell us, that we were conceited, not humble. As we progress in the Program we learn what humility is. We learn that it is trust, acceptance, honesty, and looking for the good. By asking for help from the Program we begin to learn humility. We learn not to compare ourselves to others (comparing causes feelings of superiority or inferiority and these feelings are a cover-up for the character defects within us). Our character defects cause us to feel hopeless, worthless, depressed, and anxious.

By repeated setbacks we learn humility. A whole life geared to self-centeredness cannot be set in reverse at once, but if we are willing to work for humility, that is a good start. For every one of us pain had been the admission price for this new life and the price at first was greater than expected. It brought a measure of humility which we discovered to be a healer of pain. We began to fear pain less and desire humility more.

What can we gain by being humble? Through humility, failure and misery can be transformed into priceless assets. We hear story after story of how humility has brought strength out of weakness.

Often in our illness we had an unhealthy dependency on one or more persons. We felt we could not survive without them. With humility we become aware of our dependency on God, as we understand Him. We forget ourselves and work only for the accomplishment of His will. We know we need people, not in an unhealthy dependency but realizing that a large part of our growth depends on sharing with others and building meaningful relationships.

The truly humble person is not aware that he is. If we are striving for humility, we will ask God to remove our defects. If we are ready to have them removed and believe that He will remove them, He will.

As we grow in humility, we acquire a new understanding of our God. Now, in Steps Eight and Nine, we work toward improving our relationships with other people.

STEP EIGHT

Made a list of all persons we had harmed, and became willing to make amends to them all.

When we did Step Four we included some of the wrongs we had done to others. If these guilts remain deeply buried in our minds they will cause us restless nights and wasted days. We need to be willing "to clean our own side of the fence" and take responsibility for the wrongs committed against others. From our inventory we begin to list the people we have harmed.

After taking this inventory many of us see that the person hurt the most may be ourselves. If that is the case, we make sure to include our own name on this list. Probably listed will be our spouse, family members, friends, public contacts, business associates, neighbors, or relatives.

If the list includes almost everyone we know, we must take another look at it. Some of us have been very domineering, too aggressive or sarcastic and have hurt many people. On the other hand, our self-centeredness and tendency to take things too seriously may lead us to include unnecessary names because we have exaggerated the importance of every small word or deed. In reality they probably wouldn't even know what we are talking about were we to apologize. However, we don't use this as an excuse to leave out a name. If in doubt we put down the names of all we think we have hurt and re-evaluate it when the time comes to actually make amends.

Each one of us will probably do this differently. Some of us will do the difficult ones first and some will do the easier ones first. We start with those to whom we are willing to make amends. With some on the list we are not yet ready and willing to make amends, but through prayer we continue to strive to complete all amends necessary.

Now that the list is ready, the only thing left to complete is to be willing to make amends to everyone on it which leads us to Step Nine.

STEP NINE

Made direct amends to such people wherever possible, except when to do so would injure them or others.

Now we are ready for a very difficult Step. We must go

to the people we have harmed and attempt to right these wrongs. This Step is not meant to humiliate us; it is necessary to free us from guilt and forgive us our past so we can live today.

If our own name is on the list, we may have to make amends to ourselves before we go further. We have already made a beginning by coming to the Program. Through the Program we begin to accept ourselves and develop the right attitude for making amends to others. We must not make amends expecting the same from the other person. We must take the risk - our amends may not be accepted. More likely than not, however, the amends will be well received and relationships will be improved.

Making these amends is not simply saying we are sorry. We may make amends by changing our ways of treating and dealing with others. It may require time or money, not just words, to make amends. But, if we are truly ready and willing to make them, we will not hesitate.

We do not take this Step in a hurry. It must be given proper thought and caution, but we don't procrastinate either. When we have worked Steps One through Eight in the Program, we know we are ready, and when we are ready it is time for action. If there is any doubt in our minds as to whether making amends to someone might cause harm, we consult with someone who can give an objective opinion, perhaps a Fifth Step person. We do not make amends to someone for having gossiped about that person if there is a chance he or she is not aware of the gossip. We will only hurt the person more. We do not make amends for thoughts or feelings, for these really have not hurt anyone but ourselves.

On the other hand, we don't hesitate to make amends for something which may seem ridiculous or insignificant; if the need is there, it must be done.

There may be some wrongs we can never fully right. We need not worry about them if we honestly know that we would right them if we could. Some people cannot be contacted personally. In that case we send them an honest letter or make a telephone call. If some are no longer living, the Fifth Step is the place to have made these amends. We do not delay unless there is a valid reason for postponement. In making amends we should be sensible, tactful, considerate, and humble without becoming a door mat.

If we have been painstaking about this phase of our growth:

1. We realize a new freedom and happiness.
2. We do not regret the past or wish to shut the door on it.
3. We comprehend the word serenity and we know peace of mind.
4. No matter how far down the scale we have gone we see how our experience can benefit others.
5. The feelings of uselessness and self-pity lessen.
6. We have less concern about self and gain interest in others.
7. Self-seeking slips away.
8. Our whole attitude and outlook upon life changes.
9. Our relationships with other people improve.
10. We intuitively know how to handle situations which used to baffle us.
11. We acquire a feeling of security within ourselves.
12. We realize that God is doing for us what we could not do ourselves.

These may seem like extravagant promises, but they are not. They are being fulfilled among us, sometimes quickly, sometimes slowly.

STEP TEN

*Continued to take personal inventory and when
we were wrong promptly admitted it.*

We have started to grow in awareness. Our Fourth Step inventory helped us to settle the past and then leave it behind. The Tenth Step inventory helps us to cope with daily living. We do not acquire maturity and serenity overnight, and our search for them will continue for our lifetime.

Some take their daily inventory in the morning, some in the evening; some take a spot check inventory. Our feelings tell us when it is necessary to take this inventory. If we are hurting, we need to look within. If we recognize that there is a conflict, we look for the character defect which is causing our part of the conflict. We have a choice of continuing to hang onto that which is causing our part of the conflict. We have a choice of continuing to hang onto that character defect, that hurt feeling, or replacing it with the opposite character asset.

In remembering our humanness we realize that we can fall back into our old ways of thinking and behaving. We must be willing to accept ourselves each day. We must not be discouraged if we fall short of our ideals. These disciplines are a part of our new way of life. We look for the positive things we have done each day. We cannot hang onto our negative feelings. We need to gain confidence in ourselves.

In taking our inventory we look to see if we are setting realistic goals for ourselves. Do we expect too much of others? Do we realize our human limitations and abilities? Do we let other people be human too? Are we satisfied with where we are, what we are, or what we have? Do we continue to rationalize our thoughts and feelings as an excuse not to accept what is? Do we utilize what we have learned? Have we learned to make plans and not plan the results?

In our inventory we continue to watch for self-centeredness (egotism) which causes our character defects. When this is evident, we ask God to make us willing to have it removed. If we feel the need, we discuss it with someone immediately. We make amends quickly and sincerely if we have harmed anyone. An emotional hangover can result if we procrastinate.

We cannot afford to be angry, hold resentment or self-pity. Anger can keep us off-balance and also propel us into emotional binges. It is pointless to be angry with people who also are suffering from the pains of growing. We avoid sulking or long silences. They are baited with pride and vengeance. We are sure to be happier when we accept responsibility for our actions daily and do not fall back into the pattern of blaming others.

When we feel we have failed, we promptly admit it to ourselves, and others, if necessary. Then we forgive ourselves. If we try and fail, at least we tried. It is often through our failures we learn more about ourselves. We cannot take ourselves too seriously. One of the benefits we gain is a sense of humor. We find that we can laugh at ourselves.

We ask God for help to start off the day and thank God at the end of every day for we realize that any measure of serenity has come to us by the grace of God.

STEP ELEVEN

Sought through prayer and meditation to improve our conscious contact with God as we understood Him, praying only for knowledge of His will for us and the power to carry that out.

PRAYER

In the past some of us prayed mechanically because of fear, in time of emergency, or out of a sense of duty. Some of us did not believe in God at all nor did we think that He believed in us. Some of us were very angry with God and blamed Him for our illness. In praying, sometimes we would tell God that we were failures and not worthwhile. At times we tried to bargain with Him. A lot of us have used prayer to try to change God, to get Him to do something that we wanted done. The Program shows us that prayer changes us.

Prayer is being honest about the way we really feel and going to God to ask Him to help us. We do not have to pray to God to let Him know our needs. God already knows but somehow through prayer we get in touch with ourselves as well as our Higher Power. We learn through the Program that God is a loving God and that we can go to Him as a friend.

MEDITATION

Most of us had no idea what meditation was. We had never practiced it. Meditation is trying to clear our minds of all distractions and concentrating on a truth. We spend a quiet time each day thinking about God, nature, love, the universe, a force for good, or anything that is positive. In the past we used fantasy to escape reality. Now we use our imagination in a constructive way.

When we began the Program we found it helpful to read the many books on meditation that are available. It is said that St. Francis of Assisi was practicing in the eighth century what we consider today to be the principles of the Twelve-Step Program. Many of us use his prayer for meditation, which is:

"God, make me an instrument of Thy peace;
Where there is hatred, let me sow love;
Where there is injury, pardon;
Where there is doubt, faith;
Where there is despair, hope;
Where there is darkness, light;
And where there is sadness, joy.
O Divine Master, grant that I may not seek so much to
    be consoled as to console;
To be understood, as to understand;
To be loved, as to love;
For it is in giving that we receive,
It is in pardoning that we are pardoned,
And it is in dying that we are born to eternal life."

Some of us use the Serenity Prayer:

"God grant me the serenity to accept the things I cannot change, the courage to change the things I can, and the wisdom to know the difference."

As we grow in the Program our ability to pray and meditate also grows. By setting aside a certain time for prayer and meditation each day we achieve a closer contact with God. The rewards of prayer and meditation are emotional balance and a sense of belonging.

We may experience a "dry time" when it may be difficult to pray or meditate. If we have lost contact with God, we are the ones who have removed ourselves from God. If we can accept ourselves and surrender, in time the ability to pray and meditate comes back.

GOD'S WILL

Some of us were afraid that God was going to lead us where we did not want to go. God's will does not necessarily dictate a radical change in our lives. God's will is usually taking care of the ordinary responsibilities that happen in our everyday lives. He gives us a free will to choose, and the people and the Program support us and give us confidence to make decisions. Just saying a prayer or meditating over what we cannot control can help solve a problem. Once we see something that seems right to do and appears to be God's will for us, we take action.

POWER TO CARRY THAT OUT

Sometimes we may be doubtful about God's will. We may experience crisis situations and question them. Sometimes we go to God with our wishful thinking, but we must be careful we do not rationalize and interpret our wishful thinking as Divine Guidance. We recognize the need to reach out to people. We find that it helps to consult someone, perhaps a Fifth Step person or another member. Once we feel we have some understanding of what God's will is, He will give us the power to carry it out.

STEP TWELVE

Having had a spiritual awakening as the result of these Steps, we tried to carry this message, and to practice these principles in all our affairs.

A spiritual awakening is the result of working the first Eleven Steps. We cannot make it come. It just happens. There are as many kinds of spiritual awakenings as there are people. Some people have experienced very dramatic spiritual awakenings but for most it is more subtle. It may be a recognition of our own self-worth as human beings. It may be a realization that people are there to support us, not threaten us. It may be a reassurance that there is a God. We may find that it is a combination of many things. We must not compare our spiritual awakening with those that others experience and expect more dramatic results. Each one of us must experience it in our own way.

When we have had a spiritual awakening (in whatever form it may take), we begin to realize that the promises listed on page 61 are coming true.

CARRYING THE MESSAGE

People are usually not receptive if we try to "preach" the Program rather than share our experiences. We must always be on guard to use the whole Program, not just Steps One and Twelve, or "two-stepping," as it is often called. This happens when we are afraid of the Higher Power parts of the Program so we leave out the Steps which mention God or the Steps that seem too difficult. If the Program is not working for us, perhaps we are two-stepping. The most important way we can carry the message is by example. We carry it to those who want it, not those we think need it. The importance of carrying the message is that we benefit. We grow by sharing it. A paradox of the Program is that to keep it for ourselves, we must give it away.

Some ways we can carry the message are:
1. Attending meetings and sharing with others.
2. Listening to others in the group.
3. Taking time to listen to someone on the telephone.
4. Taking the responsibility for ordering literature for the group.
5. Making coffee.
6. Starting new chapters.
7. Giving encouragement to others.
8. Writing articles for the Magazine.
9. Serving on committees.
10. Speaking on the Twelve-Step Program, when asked.

11. Providing transportation to meetings for members who have no way of getting there.
12. Making new people feel welcome before and after meetings.

We go to meetings to maintain what we have learned, to continue to grow, to share, because someone was there when *we* first came, and also in gratitude for what we have received. We always keep in mind what we were and what we are now by the grace of God.

Not everyone will accept our message and we should not be disappointed. The efforts are ours, the results are God's.

PRACTICING THE PRINCIPLES

Although we may not master the principles, we have an ideal to strive for. What is important is our daily effort. We discipline ourselves to a daily routine of practicing the Twelve Steps. It is important that we do not become complacent because our illness, like alcoholism, is only arrested, never cured. Our growth will continue the rest of our lives. After we have been in the Program for some time, the principles become a part of us. If we become complacent or indulge in some of our old thoughts, attitudes, or behavior, we sense we have not been practicing these principles and take action to bring the Program into focus again, attend an extra meeting, or make an extra phone call. We also turn to this book, read some of our other literature, and return to practicing the principles.

IN ALL OUR AFFAIRS

This is a Program of living a new way of life. It must be lived twenty-four hours a day in all aspects of our lives, such as: Home, family, social, business, financial, thought, spiritual, physical, and emotional.

CHAPTER VII

(1)

A PRISONER OF MY FEARS

My first recollection of fear was at age five. We were visiting at a house a long distance from home. I remember crouching in a corner in terror in the bedroom.

I remember running through our home screaming for my mother one dark night when a wind storm blew out all of the kerosene lamps and I felt alone.

Over a period of seven years I was in five or six tornadoes. All of our farm buildings were destroyed; all of the windows were blown out of our house and the brick house itself was cracked from chimney to basement. During those tornadoes I would kneel and pray, "God, save me and I'll be a good girl forever." And until I found the Twelve-Step Program I had a terrible fear of storms.

I was afraid of the dark, I thought there was a "boogey-man" in our upstairs storeroom, and I did not want my parents to leave me with anyone else.

We were taught that God was a punishing God and I feared misbehaving according to our family standards. I knew I was going to hell.

I had many other fears - all of them became worse as time went on - and one day when I was fifteen and a junior in high school I was called upon to read aloud. Suddenly an uncontrollable panic overwhelmed me and I could not read. From that day on I would panic whenever I was called upon to read, speak or recite. I was obsessed with the idea of, "What will people think?"

I had two brothers, no sister. My brother who was two years older than I preferred to play with a girl cousin of ours seven months older than I and they did not want me with them. I felt rejected and I was jealous and resentful.

I know now that my procrastination started when I was a little girl. I would try to escape quickly after meals so I would not have to do the dishes. I was only putting off something I knew I would have to do later.

I was born and raised on a farm on the edge of a small town. I had to work in the fields, milk cows, and feed the pigs and chickens. At age twelve I did the family washing on the washboard after school, pumping the water and heating it on the kitchen wood-burning stove. My mother had "sick headaches" during those years.

But she had a big garden, raised chickens, and canned many fruits and vegatables. She was the community midwife, always nursed the sick in our community, and there were extra out-of-work relatives staying at our house, especially in the winter, for whom she cooked and washed clothes.

I was ashamed because our house was cluttered. Now I realize there was not one closet where anything could be hung out of sight.

To provide my brothers and me with piano lessons, my mother let the teacher use the piano in our home all day to give lessons to the other children in town and she gave the teacher her lunch. In return, we received our lessons free.

I remember being ashamed because we did not have nice dinner china. We could not afford storm windows in the winter even though the temperature was sometimes 40 degrees below zero. My father put tar-paper around the foundation of our house and banked it with manure to keep the basement from freezing. I can remember being so ashamed of that manure.

My father went sheep-shearing for a couple of months each spring to supplement our small farm income. He played the violin and banjo, and one of the few fun things I remember is his teaching us to chord on the piano at age five to accompany him. He also played the piano by ear and sang many songs for us.

These were depression years and everyone in the community was poor. I was embarrassed because of my shabby shoes and my underwear made out of flour sacks, but I did not realize how poor we were until I went away to college.

Love and sex were never discussed in our home but somehow I knew that sex was "bad" and "wrong." On a few occasions when I had enough courage to ask a question, I was told that I was too young to know "that." I should not be asking "such things." I was questioned as to why I wanted to know "that" or told, "Only bad girls want to know things like 'that'."

I know my parents were the products of their upbringing and they did the best they could. They did teach us to believe in God, to be industrious and honest, to help anyone in trouble, to study hard in school, to love and respect our country, to cook, bake, sew, handle a hammer and nails, and do all kinds of farm work.

My parents were determined that all of us should go to college. I made all of my clothes, my father borrowed part of the money, and I worked two quarters for my room and board. I did not know until years later that my father and mother poured hot water over burned bread crusts to drink as coffee so they could send me money I needed at college. I seemed to be dressed well enough as I was rushed for several sororities (a status symbol) and since I was able to play the piano for singing and dancing in the dormitory, I made friends and had some feeling of being accepted. I covered my fear and panic there too.

When I entered St. Cloud State College we were required to have a minor physical examination by a doctor provided by the college. I was frightened because at the age of eighteen I had never been to a doctor. My heart beat very fast, so the doctor had me sit down for a few minutes. When he called me again he said, in jest, "Don't do what Milton Sills did this morning." (Milton Sills was a popular movie star then). I said, "What did he do?" The doctor answered, "He dropped dead this morning." I panicked. He said my heart was okay, but from that moment I started listening to my heartbeat. I knew there must be something wrong.

I do not know how I ever finished college. I would refrain from reciting rather than speak in class. I suffered terrible panic all the time. And traveling on the bus to and from college was torture.

We had lost our farm by mortgage foreclosure, something which happened to many during the depression. I always feared the talk of poverty and bills owed.

The winter after we lost our farm, we moved into a house in the neighboring town. My father had no work, both my brothers were at home, one with a wife and baby, and they had no work. I was eighteen years old, had completed one year of college and was teaching a rural school out in the country. I had to walk two miles each way every day. My teaching salary of $85.00 a month was the only income for the whole family that winter. I can remember feeling resentment during that time. Two years after the 1929 crash my father bought back the same farm we had lost for a small price because property values had fallen so low.

My first teaching position after going back to college was in a town of about three thousand in west-central Minnesota. It was during the years of the infamous dust storms. During the day it would be as black as night from the dust-filled air. We would close all the windows and go to bed with wet cloths over our faces. In the morning the window ledges would have an inch of fine dust which had sifted in. If it rained at all it rained mud. In my fear and panic I thought the end of the world was coming and that I would never again breathe fresh air.

I taught school for two and one-half years, married at age twenty-two and was divorced within two years. In those days school teachers were a "dime a dozen" and our contracts stated that we could not be married. A divorced woman was never considered for a position as a school teacher. So I went to the city in which I now live to look for a job. I found what was considered a good job in those days. Several years later I met my present husband and married him after two years of "going together."

I also found a doctor who prescribed barbiturates for me. I took them for about ten years. Then came the "miraculous" tranquilizers. I had Valium, Librium, Thorazine and Equinil, anti-depressants such as Stellazine, diet pills such as Praeludin and Desoxyn, and the time-release amphetamines. This continued for another fifteen years. I drank socially. The pills did not seem to lessen my fears, but I learned that a couple of drinks on top of the pills would help me forget my fears for a little while. I did not know the danger of combining pills and alcohol then.

My fears had become progressively worse. I now had pains in my chest, dizziness, roaring in my ears (I thought I was having a stroke), I couldn't swallow, couldn't take a deep breath; I could not go anywhere, could not drive my car; I could not be in an elevator, go through a tunnel, or be in deep woods; and an airplane was out of the question. I developed ulcers.

I could not be at home alone. Then I had panic when my family was with me. I would say to myself, "You are warm, you are fed, you are clothed, you have a nice home, you are well, your husband and children are with you - so why are you full of panic?" I did not know why.

For the first ten years after I met my present husband I did not tell him of my fears. I would lie to him, giving some other excuse for not going some place. And when I did tell him it was very hard for him to understand because he had never experienced that kind of fear and panic.

I was not permitted to see a psychiatrist because in our family we were supposed to be "adult" and solve our own problems. Seeing a psychiatrist had not yet become a status symbol either.

My resentment, anger, and self-pity were also becoming a problem. My father was bedridden at our home for a year and three months, and after his death my mother continued to live with us. Shortly afterward my mother-in-law died, and my father-in-law came to live with us. He lived with us for nine years. We have two children; one was an infant and one was six years old when my father and mother first came to our house. We had four bedrooms so I had to sleep on a bed davenport in the den. There was only an archway - no privacy.

We have our business office at home and I did all of my husband's book work. Because of our children I became involved in Camp Fire, Boy Scouts, church, and school affairs. I enjoyed these activities even though I was overcome with panic most of the time.

At least once a week I would lash out at the whole household, yelling, swearing and saying the grandparents could just leave our house, knowing all the time there was no other place for them to go.

I blamed everyone else and everything else for the way I was. And how I hated myself for behaving the way I did! I felt as if I were on a train going down a railroad track with no brakes and I didn't know how to stop. I had such guilt feelings. Since I had been brought up to believe God was a punishing God, I feared Him and I feared death. I was so miserable I wanted to die, but I knew I would go to hell so I couldn't die.

In the meantime, my doctor had finally convinced me that I had no heart trouble, and he also told me that in my severest panic the worst thing that could happen would be that I would pass out. My body would then automatically relax and I would regain consciousness - and so what? Someone would look for identification and take me home. The only thing that might be hurt would be my pride. His comments comforted me. I thank God that my doctor has been like the old-time family doctor who sits and talks to his patients. He told me twenty-seven years ago that sixty percent of his patients' illnesses were caused by emotions rather than anything organic. He was years ahead of many doctors in admitting that.

On October 31, 1965, in our local Sunday newspaper an article appeared which told about the Twelve-Step Program of Alcoholics Anonymous having been adapted for persons with emotional problems. I read it and I knew at once that this was something I must have.

There were no local chapters in our area and I knew I would not be finished with my commitments in church, school, Camp Fire Girls and Boy Scouts until the next fall (1966). I thought to myself, "If there is no group in existence here by that time, maybe I can start one."

But, as I have seen hundreds of times in the Twelve-Step Program, my Higher Power (God) stepped in.

The following February (1966) a friend of mine invited me to attend some Al-Anon orientation sessions with her. There was an alcoholic in her family and, since we were good friends, she wanted me to learn something about the disease of alcoholism so that my husband and I might better understand.

I went with her and discovered that the Twelve Steps of the Al-Anon Program were exactly the same as those I had read about in the newspaper article. I continued to go to regular weekly meetings with my friend. She helped me to learn how to apply the Steps to my life and within two months I had made progress noticeable enough for my doctor to say, "Why do you wait to start a chapter here? Why don't you do it right away?"

Since my panic would not permit me to go far from home I had to look for a meeting place nearby. There was a community center in the park behind our house. I called the director for an appointment. My heart was beating hard as I talked to him. He listened and then said we could meet there. I thank God that he was receptive to this new concept of helping persons with emotional problems.

I talked to my Al-Anon friends and they said they would come to the meetings for a while. Some of them continued to come for several months until we could get along without their assistance.

So the first chapter in the upper midwest of what is now Emotions Anonymous started in St. Paul, Minnesota on April 13, 1966.

At that first meeting about twelve persons were present. The existence of the group reached the news media and articles appeared in newspapers in St. Paul and Minneapolis.

The following week there were over sixty-five persons present and I felt I had a tiger by the tail.

Attendance continued in large numbers and that fall of 1966 a member started a chapter in Minneapolis. We were surprised when another sixty-five persons attended.

Other groups sprang up in these two cities and their suburbs and around Minnesota. Within five years there were more than thirty groups in our state. From these, more chapters started in neighboring states.

As has already been stated in the Chapter on HOW IT STARTED, a feeling had developed among members in our state, a few other states, and in one foreign country that we should disassociate from the organization with which we were affiliated and start our own fellowship under another name. The name "EMOTIONS ANONYMOUS" was chosen and permission to adapt the Twelve Steps of AA for our use was granted by A. A. World Services, Inc. The people and the Program remained the same — only the name and the administration of the fellowship have been changed.

As I look back now I believe the first fifty-four years of my life held a combination of feelings of fear, anger, anxiety, inferiority, inadequacy, false arrogance, false pride, pretense, self-pity, resentment, and envy. And until I started to practice the Twelve-Step Program in February of 1966, I did not know just how emotionally ill I was. I never knew who I was and I never felt any self-worth. I never felt I belonged. I always tried to do extra things for others to prove myself worthy or to please others.

The first thing the Twelve-Step Program taught me was that my Higher Power is a loving God, not a punishing God. I always prayed wildly, "God, help me - God, help me!" Now I talk to God as a friend. I am not afraid of Him. He is a loving Friend who is with me all of the time and on Whom I call several times a day; and since I feel okay with God, I am not as sensitive to any gossip or criticism from others.

Within six months all of my fears and panic were gone. I was out of my personal prison after forty years of suffering. I can go any place now, drive my car, be in elevators, tunnels or deep woods, or travel alone by airplane. I can be in a crowd, I can sit in a large audience without having to sit by the door so I can get out in a hurry, and I can speak in public (even on radio and TV — for EA). Within that same six months I was able to be off all mind and mood-altering pills and I have had none for the past eleven years.

The crippling, destructive anger, resentment, and self-pity are gone. If they recur, they do not last long and are not severe. I have the tools of our Program to deal with them. I feel a sense of self-worth. I do not have to prove myself to anyone. I do not have to always be right. People do not have to agree with me, nor do I have to agree with everyone else. I have dispensed with false pride, pretense, putting on a front, and abnormal feelings of inadequacy.

I am able to be more patient and to show my family and my ninety-seven-year-old mother, who still lives with us, that I love them. My father-in-law died at our house five years ago.

I believe that my life was planned to bring me to the Twelve-Step Program so that I might find the beautiful close contact which I now have with God.

I used to think I had what I called "lesser" character defects such as procrastination and overweight. I now believe there is no character defect which is lesser or greater. I believe that all of my defects are equally serious, whether they affect others or me.

Last year we had a fire in our home while I was at the hospital with my husband who was undergoing surgery. The damage to our house and contents amounted to more than $71,000. Because of my procrastination I had not completed taking pictures of the interior of our home and listing special antiques and other pieces. After the fire it was impossible to verify the loss of many things. I no longer look upon procrastination as a lesser character defect. It was a costly one.

Most of the time I can accept myself as I am *today* -- that is important to me. What I was *yesterday* is past and what I might be *tomorrow* or in the future is in God's hands.

Each day I strive for the humility to do God's will in all things.

In 1971 two EA members talked to me about taking a course in Chemical Dependency Counseling at the University of Minnesota. I had not been in college for over thirty-five years and I did not know if I could study again. I applied for admittance and was accepted. I passed the course requirements and served an internship in a treatment center, a women's halfway house, and worked with chemically dependent senior citizens. Because I had started the first chapter in the upper midwest of what is now Emotions Anonymous, and because of my experience in organizing, and my time in the Program, the required number of days of internship was cut from one-hundred-fifty working days to seventy-four working days. I was in my early sixties when I received my certificate from the university as a chemical dependency counselor. I was fortunate to obtain a position as counselor in a halfway house for men. I worked there one year and then realized that I could not accept money for helping someone else when I had received the Twelve-Step Program free. I resigned and am happy sharing with fellow Twelve-Step Program members, working on committees and in our EA international office as a volunteer. Later I did go back to that halfway house for a few months as Interim Program Director until a permanent one could be found. I have also continued taking other specialized courses at the University of Minnesota such as Advanced Group Process Techniques, Family Counseling, and Adult Psychology for Mental Health Workers. These, too, are among the many miracles which have happened in my life because of the Twelve-Step Program.

I plan to continue attending EA meetings regularly as long as I am able and to practice this beautiful way of life as long as I live. By attending meetings and working the EA program every day to the best of my ability I am more able to maintain what I have learned. Without regular attendance at meetings I know I would slip back into my old ways. We know the paradox that we cannot keep what we have unless we give it away, so I want to be at meetings when new people come seeking help, just as those beautiful Al-Anon members were there when I came for the first time.

I cannot end my story without giving credit to my wonderful husband and my children. My husband has encouraged and supported me all the way in my progress in the Program. He has allowed me free rein with time, money, a car, absence from home to attend chapter and committee meetings, or to travel on public speaking engagements for the Program.

The main office was in our home for eight years and before we had an answering service there were as many as forty telephone calls a day. There were many, many committee meetings in our home. Members have always been welcome to spend a day, overnight, or longer with us. I can provide coffee, cold drinks and food for EA members. When several members have had to travel many miles away to speak for EA, my husband has gone along to drive our car so the rest of us could relax before and after speaking. To me this is his way of thanking EA for what it has done for me and for our family. And I thank God every day that I am his wife.

My children, who are now twenty-two and twenty-eight, have been pleasant and helpful when members are in our home. They, too, appreciate the change in me and my different attitudes and actions toward them. My daughter is married and no longer lives at home and my son will be leaving next spring to be married.

We are very proud of both of them. They have grown up to be admirable persons. We also have good relationships with and love the persons they have chosen as their life-mates. I say now they turned out well in spite of me, not because of me, and I thank God every day.

I know that my life and the lives of my family are completely in the hands of God. Every day I thank Him for bringing me to this beautiful Program and for the wonderful, loyal friends I have found in EA.

What a good feeling it is to "Let go and let God."

Marion

A GREAT CONTROLLER

I came into the Twelve-Step Program in December of 1966. I had been under psychiatric care since 1954. This involved visits to the psychiatrist a minimum of once a week for twelve years. In 1961 I was hospitalized one month for nerves. In December of 1963, I entered the hospital and stayed seven months, taking tranquilizers and anti-depressants the whole time.

When I first came to the meetings, I was unable to open my mouth and say anything. I had a hard time understanding what was meant by surrender.

The concept of a Higher Power was repugnant to me. I had been raised in a strict religion. God to me was a bearded grandfather who sat on a cloud making black marks in a book about me. I was damned, in my opinion!

In 1950 I had given birth to a handicapped child. I felt at first it was my punishment but I did not know for what I was being punished. As time went on, I became very angry with God and so I rejected Him.

A funny thing happened when I lost belief in a Higher Power. I then had to become my own Higher Power. With no concept of anyone outside myself who cared, I became the "great controller." I almost had to sleep with my feet in the air to keep the sky from falling.

All of my life I had been looking for rules to live by. The school, church, or family didn't give me a satisfactory knowledge of how to live in the cruel terrifying world. Then I read the Twelve Steps! Slowly, as my anxieties diminished, I was able to understand the Steps.

Attending the meetings and listening to others helped in this process. But it was about three or four years before I felt I was able to work the Program. That is why I tell new people to "keep coming back."

The Fifth Step was crucial to me. As a neurotic I spent my life avoiding commitment. The Fifth Step was my commitment to this Program. I gave myself totally to the EA way of life with my first Fifth Step.

For me personally, I know there is no cure for my neurosis. I intend to continue coming to meetings the rest of my life or until two days after I'm dead.

Like the alcoholic, I must be aware daily of my limitations. Certain stresses and strains can still throw me back to my old ways, but the Steps and the meetings are the tools I use to work out of it.

Fearful control was the root of my neurosis. I lived in torment for years. My release has come by working the Steps.

I find the AA term H.A.L.T. to be a tool I use every day to warn me of trouble brewing. H.A.L.T. stands for hungry, angry, lonely, and tired. Any one of these four factors can toss me into depression. I then must pinpoint what factor is working against me and do something about it.

I am afraid of people and fearful of criticism. I must work daily on this because I have seen where this has hurt not only me but EA as a whole. Not wanting to be involved or to be hurt has kept me quiet when I should have been involved. My repressed anger has come spurting out at inappropriate times. Such behavior is neurotic, but EA has given me new life. Without it I would be dead by now, a hopeless suicide, but with the help of the Twelve Steps and my Higher Power, I am not.

Jackie

(3)

THERE WAS WARMTH AND ACCEPTANCE
IN THAT LITTLE ROOM

I came to my first Twelve-Step meeting by accident in the fall of 1966. I was bringing a friend who needed to go. I came back a couple more times to bring my friend, but I soon saw the Program was what I was looking for. This was in the very early days; I think the group was only the second one formed. So everyone there was struggling to understand the Program himself. But there was a warmth and acceptance in that little room in that church basement that was like coming home. It was like walking into a warm room on a cold winter day.

I remember at one of those first meetings asking Ann why I felt so good there. She looked at me with those big blue eyes of hers and said, "That's because we accept you, Jesse."

There were other times when things didn't go so well. I would find myself listening to a couple of women worrying how they could get through the day. Here I was very successfully getting a Ph.D. in psychology and teaching. I would think, "What am I doing with this bunch of neurotic housewives?"

I remember one of these conversations well. One woman was saying she didn't know how she could make it through the day. One of the other women told her how she handled the same problem. She would look at the clock and if it was 10:20 in the morning, she would concentrate on making it to 10:25, just five minutes at a time. I thought how awful it must be to be that desperate. It took me some years to see that five minutes at a time was a good way to live. It was especially helpful when the going got rough.

What kept me coming to the meetings for some time was the acceptance I found, the relief I felt to be able to voice my feelings. It was a long time before I came to see how powerless over my emotions I was. And it was way longer before I saw any need to be restored to sanity. Sanity was something some of the other members needed but it certainly didn't apply to me. I was always at work on time. After a while I was able to admit that my overdriven life was maybe a little mixed up but not insane. It was just in the last few years that I finally saw how insane I really was in the way I was living my life. I would do almost anything for anyone who could help me look bigger and more important in the eyes of my fellow man and I nearly killed myself doing it.

A little bit of surrender came into my life and even that little bit was a vast improvement. Before I had my heart attack in 1962, I vowed that I would never again do anything I didn't believe in. As I started to search for what I believed in, I saw how often I didn't know what was right for me. I tried psychiatry, figuring a guy who could have a heart attack by the time he was thirty-five must have some problems. But that didn't work for me because I couldn't and wouldn't tell the psychiatrist what I really felt.

When I came to EA, I found the Program and principles and the examples of peoples' lives to be what I had been looking for and only finding in bits and pieces up to that time. So I went at the Program diligently. I would be angry at some person who came to meetings and never talked about the Steps. I feel now that the Program works a lot by osmosis; the parts that were most important to me, I got, not by working hard on them but more by their sinking in as I sat in the meetings, and got the feeling of the meetings and watched the expressions on peoples' faces.

I wrote out Step Four fairly early. I figured my Fifth Step was so bad that only a priest could hear it. Anyone else would turn to stone. Since then, I've done Four and

Five many, many times. That first Fourth Step just scratched the surface, but it was necessary as a start so I could get closer to the real problems that lay so much deeper.

I moved to Montana in the summer of 1967 and was part of a group there where some folks from AA helped us get going. After a couple of years of meetings, a badly crippled man came to a meeting and blew up in a rage at everyone there. That, plus some difficulties we had with a few members who had some severe mental problems, broke up the meeting for four years.

Eventually I saw that I needed meetings again and started going to the AA open meeting on Sunday with a couple of AA's. Then in 1973 EA was started up again and I went to that, too.

An old AA friend says, "We will bandage up a sick toe but we won't do anything about our sickness of the mind." I've seen that in myself so much. But now that I've spent more time in meetings, I've come to see that the times when things are going well are the best times to work on my problems so when the crises come, there is more to work with.

Our Program has given me a sense of peace in my daily life that I didn't know existed. It has taken away my loneliness. I used to be lonely even in the midst of a group. When I was by myself, I could be terribly lonely. I'm not lonely any more. And I am beginning to be able to love myself and a few other people enough so that I have some friends who like me the way I am. All this has made my life far lovelier than I ever could have imagined. And it has given me the strength I've needed to accept some of the problems I have had to face in life. Most all of this has come from our Twelve Steps and you lovely people who have taught them to me.

Jesse

(4)

EMOTIONAL PROBLEMS CAUSE UNHAPPINESS

I don't know what caused my emotional problems or when they started, but they have been with me all of my life. I can't remember a time before this Program that I had any sustained periods of happiness. My first memories were that something was wrong, but I was unable to put my finger on it or really describe it.

For what I lacked in happiness I made up for in faith. I always believed that happiness was just around the corner or over the next hill. I believed that when something changed, or I did something, I was going to be happy. I chased this illusion for thirty-three years.

At first I thought that happiness must lie in going to school. The older kids who were going to school looked happy so I concluded that when I got old enough to go to school I would be happy, too. Well, I went to school but I did not become happy.

I was always on the track of happiness and always watching for anything that might relieve this feeling that I had. Much conversation that I heard centered around money. It seemed that everyone that I talked to said that money was the key to happiness. That was not such a great problem. There is always work to be done and children can get money. Before I was ten years old I knew that money would not be a source of happiness for me. I would get it, spend it, and end up no happier, so that was one more door that closed on me.

The world is full of publicity that tells us that

romance is the key to happiness, so I had a go at that, too. Although I was not unhappy with romance and did enjoy it, it did not remove that feeling that all was not right with me. I still couldn't find the key.

As I grew older I thought that freedom might be the key that would unlock the door of happiness for me. After I learned a profession I moved out of state, hoping that a change would make me happy. After working in Michigan, Wisconsin, and South Dakota, I returned to my home state, Minnesota, no happier than before. So geographical changes did not work for me. Another door had closed.

I joined clubs and organizations in a search for peace of mind. None of these seemed to be able to break the barrier and things got no better for me. I couldn't understand how others managed to be so happy, and I remained so miserable.

Next I gave marriage a try. Although I was not unhappy with marriage and found that it had much to offer, it still did not give me the answer I was looking for. I bought a house, settled down, and started to raise a family, and for about five years was somewhat stable. However, the feeling of things not being right did not leave me.

After five years I decided to try a change in jobs and locations again. The moves and the changes had no permanent effect on me and my emotional problems followed me and seemed to dominate all areas of my life. Everywhere I went I felt like an outcast who did not belong.

The turning point in my life came nine years ago. I had taken a look at myself. I was thirty-three years old, was educated, had a profession, had a home, had a family, and nothing to look forward to but getting old. And I was just as unhappy as the first day of my life that I could remember. I had tried everything that society said was supposed to make people happy, but I was miserable. I had concluded that happiness was just a word in the dictionary and did not really exist.

The change for me came in the summer of 1967. A

Twelve-Step Program started in the town where I lived, that was pointed toward persons with problems other than alcoholism. I was invited to join and have been attending ever since.

I was one of the fortunate ones because the Program started to work for me at the first meeting, and it has been working ever since. Since it has been working for nine years, I have faith that it is no "flash in the pan" thing.

At this writing it is almost hard to remember how bad it was. I do remember that the meetings were on Monday nights at a church, and in the beginning I used to "hang on" from meeting to meeting by telling myself, "It's almost Monday; you can make it."

These meetings were a do-or-die thing with me. Everything I had tried for serenity had not worked and I was at the end of things to try. In this case it was really necessary that I put my all into it because I did feel that this was probably my last chance for happiness.

I promised myself that if this recovery program did not work, it was not going to be because I did not give it a try. I promised myself that I would try to do everything that was suggested to the best of my ability. I tried to live the Program day and night.

In the beginning I was quite confused about this recovery Program and what was expected of me. I could see no relationship between the Steps and I could not even understand what they meant. I knew what the words meant, but I was not able to relate them to me or my emotional problems.

The thing that kept me coming back to the meetings was that I liked the people and I liked what they said. There was a feeling at the meetings that something was happening. For the first time in my life I felt truly at home. Here I felt accepted.

What I liked about the Program was that I felt that there was a genuine interest in me and my problems. I lost the feeling that people were trying to change me for their own ends. Before, I always felt that others wanted me to change to satisfy some desire in themselves. Here I felt that they wanted me to change so that I would be happy.

I was told that my recovery would be all up to me. I could attend meetings, or not attend; it was up to me. I could practice the Program or not practice it. I could contribute or not contribute. What I did I would be doing on my own. No one was going to be looking over my shoulder and checking up on me and keeping a record of my progress. If I wanted to get well, I was told that I was going to have to work at it, and work at it hard. About the only thing I could expect was encouragement and a few suggestions.

I found out that I was allowed to talk about only the problems I suffered from and what I was doing about them. I couldn't talk about anyone or anything else.

In the beginning I could only understand a few of the Steps. I was told to work on those I could understand and apply, and the rest would reveal themselves at the proper time. Steps Four and Ten were two that I felt that I could handle, so I started with those. At meetings, other Steps were discussed and I did my best to understand them, but put most of my own efforts on applying Steps Four and Ten.

As time passed I was able to understand more and more of the Steps. As I was able to understand them emotionally I was able to apply them to my life and my problems. As the years rolled by, more and more of the Steps were at my command to help me combat my emotional illness.

In this last year I was finally able to come to terms with Steps Eight and Nine. I just could not seem to figure out exactly how to go about applying these Steps. Then one day at a meeting the discussion was on Step Nine. As it was with several of the other Steps, the meaning came to me as if someone had turned on a light. What I had been struggling to understand was finally clear to me. I was now able to see how I could apply Steps Eight and Nine to my recovery.

I joined this Program because I was unhappy. In this

Program I learned that the only one who can make me happy is myself.   My parents can't do it or couldn't do it because they were too busy being parents.   The school couldn't do it because they were too busy teaching.   Money could not make me happy because all it is is a method of exchange.   My whole life was spent trying to find happiness in the wrong places.

I learned about true happiness in Step Eleven and the Prayer of St. Francis.   It says, "'Tis better to love than be loved."   I now realize that if I am doing the loving it can never be turned off.   It says, "'Tis better to give than to receive."   If I am receiving, my happiness is dependent on what someone else does, but if I am doing the giving, then my happiness can never be stopped.   This can be applied in line after line in that Prayer.

The most wonderful thing about this Program is that it works.   I had tried so many things before that ended up in failure.   I came to this Program because I was unhappy. Through the Program my unhappiness has been changed to happiness,   and   for   this   I   shall   be   forever   grateful.

Dave

(5)

GOD'S DETOURS

Life is a series of roads which lead to various goals. A road cannot be chosen until one goal is selected. Many different roads end at the same goal. Without a plan, man doesn't reach any destination, yet he keeps on going on. I was an individual who lacked a goal, a plan, or a reason for just going on, and I did not have the faintest idea what to do about it.

I was a very physically ill person. My illness started as canker sores in my mouth, followed by swollen gums, mouth and lips that blistered, cracked, and became skinless, a red, sensitive tongue, bags under my eyes, and jowls that hung. With the swollen mouth condition, I became unable to enunciate sufficiently to take phone calls. Eating was more difficult. I could not drink from a glass or straw, as they would adhere to my skinless lips. So I fed myself like a bird does her babies — pouring it from on high. My weight went down to ninety pounds. Similar irritations lined my stomach. It hurt equally whether I ate or not. Self diagnosis told me — cancer or ulcers.

Because I looked like a leper, everyone stared and flooded me with questions. I refused to leave the house socially. When it was a necessity, I faked a cough, holding a large handkerchief over my mouth. Well-meaning friends offered remedies and advice. It caused pain and effort to explain the treatments I was undergoing.

Three days a week, for three months, I visited my family doctor who gave shots and painted my mouth and lips with prescribed medication. To ease the pain, I folded my arms across my abdomen. Nights offered no release. What if a sheet or pillow would touch my lips? Even though they were heavy with ointment, they adhered together during my sleep. It required a hot pack to open them. I had problems getting to sleep until my doctor prescribed sleeping pills. Then during sleep my body began to twitch and the doctor gave me nerve pills.

Sometimes I awakened with abdominal spasms which required a shot to relieve. My condition was gradually worsening; medical science could not help me.

My Higher Power finally came to my rescue when I became a hopeless victim of my circumstances. I lost a filling from a tooth. My dentist could not help me because I could not open my mouth. He was appalled at my condition and sent me to an oral surgeon. The specialist's diagnosis was, "No physical cause, just the result of tension; don't return to your family doctor; discontinue all medications, your body is allergic to same; take warm salt-soda mouthwashes hourly, and get rid of tension." I understood mouthwashes, but I did not have the foggiest notion of how to get rid of tensions.

My husband was a problem drinker. Without any training, I understood neither alcoholism nor emotional problems, so I blamed my mate for my illness. Finally my husband decided we would go to AA. In less than a year he quit, but I continued in Al-Anon for a longer period. There was no local group, so I had to travel far, risk icy winter roads, and travel with a car pool of men. Discouraged, I also quit. However, it was enlightening to learn that I had not caused his drinking and I was not responsible for his sobriety.

My psychosomatic symptoms were my first detour signs on the road to serenity. I needed them to alert me to change my habits of thinking and acting. Al-Anon was my first Twelve-Step experience. My Higher Power kept posting additional Twelve-Step detour signs along my path. At this time I was a Family Affairs Commissioner of twenty communities. The chairman invited me to a workshop on family programs. It was conducted by a psychiatrist's wife who introduced us to Emotions Anonymous. Because it was another Twelve-Step Program, I was impressed with it and felt at home. These ideas were important for I could present them in my local workshops. However, I didn't think any of my people would have use for such a Program because I thought emotional problems were found only in large cities. So my Higher Power had to put out another detour sign.

When we were visiting my husband's niece, she mentioned that her brother-in-law was having nerve problems and was involved in the same Program. I had never seen any literature, not did I know where to get it. Since it was an anonymous group, I did not dare let him know I knew he was associated with it. Instead, I wrote him of my involvement with family affairs and asked how I might obtain some EA material for my workshop. He surprised me with a complete packet which I read and shelved for the future.

Many months later another detour sign appeared. Early one morning, a professional friend approached me after becoming very upset because of a breakdown in the presence of her clients on the previous day. She never wanted to return to her work again, as no one would have confidence in her. Our conversation centered around consoling her. I forgot about my EA material until she left. Quickly I followed her and explained the packet. Her reaction was, "I am very interested in this, because I'm on anti-depressants which leave me more depressed. But before making a decision, I want my husband's opinion." At that moment her husband arrived, having become ill at work. This afforded me the opportunity to personally explain EA. He too was intrigued, but would make no commitment until he obtained some recommendation from his family doctor, whom he was on his way to visit. That doctor endorsed it and encouraged them to participate.

God worked through my friend in setting up another sign for my detour. Both she and her husband began making one-hundred-thirty mile weekly trips to the nearest EA group and found them very satisfying. One night her husband had to work, so she asked me to accompany her. This was a great opportunity to see this group in action for I had long wondered what a whole room of neurotics looked like. What a surprise to find they looked no different than the shoppers I met everyday at the grocer's. She invited me about nine times that summer, but my pride would not let me share my real feelings with my friend or her group. When my turn came to contribute to the discussions, I responded, "I am xxxxx, and I am a companion to my friend." With each additional meeting, my enthusiasm about EA increased. It would be the highlight of my fall workshops! I could see that many of my friends and relatives could use the Program, but through my Higher Power I began to see how good EA was for me, too.

My conscience began to gnaw at me. "Isn't it selfish that you and two friends should be the only ones who are aware of EA in one quarter of the state?" Thus, when my church group was revamping its schedule, I suggested that our program chairman present EA. She not only took my suggestion, but she invited ladies of all our town's churches to share the program. Later a woman approached me questioningly. "Why do we have to travel so far to a group? Why can't we have a local chapter? Several of us are interested. How many do we need to start?" That did it! We started with an Open Meeting the following week, and there has been a weekly meeting in our town ever since. It amazed me how God has had to repeatedly work through other people to divert me from my old ways into the detours to improve myself.

My friend decided she would continue meeting with her original city group. That left me as the only local person to ever witness the Twelve-Step meeting in action. I had been using the ideas that I had previously picked up at meetings and was applying them to my life. But now I had a greater responsibility — to lead a new group. That was an incentive to work the Program all the harder. To better understand the Program, I read all the available Twelve-Step literature.

Also, some of my old physical symptoms were returning, indicating to me that a character defect was surfacing. I am grateful for symptoms. They are alarms that go off when I am regressing. Without them I could easily slip back into all my old habits of negativeness. It became evident that I could not drop the Program after my symptoms were gone. I needed it for maintenance insurance to prevent them from recurring.

Such phrases as, "You can't keep it unless you give it away," impressed me. But I realized I couldn't give it away until I had it myself. Finally I was ready to present EA in my Family Affairs workshops, and I did. Our new EA group grew in size and maturity. Word of it spread into surrounding communities. Gradually we were invited to tell about EA to many organizations, service clubs, church groups, and schools (with the permission of the International Office), experiences which helped us to mature and do Twelfth Step work. The longer I am in the Program, the harder I work it. Maybe I understand it better, but mostly it is because I need it and want more of what it gives. When I become lax in it, life still goes on, but the inner peace is gone. I am left all tied up inside.

Up to this point I was the only family member attending EA. The more I worked on Step Four, the greater was the realization that my character defects were rooted in infancy. We had a five-year-old son who was an extrovert, displaying many negative traits. The child was becoming a victim of his environment, living in a family with emotions that were poorly handled. I was constantly wishing he had my Program. I talked about it at my EA group, but I could not find any interest there. One does not start a group for one child. But my beautiful, loving, and perceptive Higher Power was right there with His sign posts once more, showing me the way.

Members of our group were leaving to attend a weekend Twelve-Step Retreat eighty miles distant. A lady who drove one-hundred-thirty miles weekly to attend our meetings until she was able to start her own group, arrived by bus and joined us for the trip. I shared my desire for a children's EA group; so did she. Before we arrived at the retreat, she suggested, "If you start the group, I will bring our children to your group each week." Even though the next Saturday was Easter Saturday, we chose it for our first meeting with seven little members present. Our Children's Emotions Anonymous group is seven years old now and still functioning. Older brothers and sisters of our CEAers decided they wanted a group, also. So that August, we started a Youth Emotions Anonymous. A little girl who attended our first CEA meeting, is now a teenager and belongs to our YEA group. Another YEA member has had two years of CEA, has three brothers and sisters in CEA, and her parents are in EA — a Twelve-Step family! Three YEAers come sixty miles weekly and their families don't have a car. Where there's a will, there's a way! They never miss a meeting, even when the temperature is thirty-five degrees below zero.

Others who have wanted YEA have also made sacrifices. My out-of-state niece, who was attending a boarding high school fifty miles from here, wanted to be part of our YEA. She arranged with students from her local college who were commuting from my town for transportation weekly to YEA. While she was in college, she wrote a term paper on EA. Other students have done the same.

Gradually, people close to me were being involved in EA. But by the time YEA started, my older son was off to college. He attended enough meetings to know what it was all about. Without being conscious of it, he seems to be coping with problems by using the EA philosophy. One night my husband surprised me by saying, "I think I'll go along to your meeting this evening." He continued in the group for about a year. I never heckled him into going. He would have to *want* to go if he were to get anything out of EA. People often ask me how long I plan to stay in EA. With the grace of God I hope I can be in it all my life. If I ever have to move to a place where there is no EA group, first I shall unpack the groceries, then start an EA group, after which I shall be sufficiently relaxed to hang the drapes. There is no experience in my pre-EA life that I wish to repeat. I am happier now than I have been in my whole life. Yet nothing has changed. I live in the same town, same house, with the same family. All that is different is myself, my habits, attitudes, thinking, priorities, and many character traits. I know that I was the author of my own illness ten years ago, letting tense situations get through to me. Many more traumatic events came into my life since I came into EA: Serious accidents, near deaths, deaths, serious illnesses, loss of jobs, and family breakups. Through them there remained that inner peace, no panic, fears, worries, or anxieties. Why?

The key to why or how EA works for me is my Higher Power. It is not new to have one; He has always been part of my faith. What is new about Him is my feeling about Him and our relationship. I used to place Him on a throne on a high cloud to rule His world. Our Sunday encounter was foreign, cold, and impersonal. When in dire need, I screamed for help and wondered IF He would help. My God now is the same one I always had, but our relationship has changed. Through working the Eleventh step, I know Him better. My conscious contact with Him is constantly improving; that is my KEY.

The way I pray is different, too. I quit praying for the material things I once wanted for happiness because they didn't change my feelings after I obtained them. I seldom ask anything for myself. Since I have serenity, what else do I need? I pray that "hurting people" will find EA and serenity, and a closer relationship with their Higher Power. When praying for myself or others, I add these phrases: "Please, God, if it is Your will; if it is not, substitute what is better; do it in Your own way and in Your own time." If I did not obtain my request, I used to figure God did not answer my prayer. But now I feel that no prayer goes unanswered, although the answer may take a form that we do not recognize. Now when I pray for something, in the next breath I thank God for starting the wheels in motion, even though the answer may take a lifetime.

Once I thought that the criteria for being a good parent was to worry and fret about the children when they were out of sight. That certainly did not help them any. Sometimes I think that my children aren't really mine but God's, and He is just lending them to me to take care of. He will give me all the help I need to carry out this mission, if I just take the time to ask. I completely "let go" of my children and put them entirely in God's competent hands.. I now use my thinking and time for things I can do something about.

Gradually, I am learning to stop giving advice and directives to others. Letting go of the lives of people has been a difficult task. Every time I had the urge to interfere, I would say to myself, "Mind your own business." It took much practice in self-discipline. Being human, I do slip back into my old negative ways, but I now concentrate on doing the right thing. The present is all the time I have. "Please, God, remove this character defect. Help me control my emotions instead of letting my emotions control me."

To make God a habit is my present aim. When I remember to do all thing with Him, I have no problem. I must practice doing the little things with Him or surely I'll not remember the difficult ones. When I used to do things on my own and they did not work out right, I became very discouraged. But when I do them with God and the tasks fail, I assume they were not supposed to happen. Now I ask God to post detour signs to keep me off the negative roads. The detour is the EA way. I don't always have the wisdom or the courage to chance the new detour which appears hard to use and is less traveled. Before I had enough EA experience, I passed many signs because I did not understand their meaning. Step Three shows me the answer — to want to do God's will and ask Him for the wisdom and courage to carry it out.

I have made a commitment to myself to never miss a weekly EA meeting, except for serious illness or extreme emergencies. Right after every meeting I get the feeling that I could handle all the problems of the world. This strength does drain as I continue to cope with my problems. Most weeks I attend four meetings. As each member shares the way he works EA, I am collecting a tool to use as the need arises. The more meetings I attend, the more tools I have. THE CHOICE IS MINE. I thank God for His detour signs which showed me the way to EA and His will for me, and the beautiful friends He put in my life.

Anonymous

(6)

A LITTLE BOY GROWS UP

As a young boy I was dissatisfied. Even though I lived in a family where everybody, my grandparents, my parents, and my younger brother, cared much for me, I was searching for something - I didn't know what. It seemed as if there were something I had to find. I had a feeling of dis-ease with the world.

When I was young, there were many sick people in my family, including my mother, who was operated on at one time. I saw a lot of hospitals from the inside and met many doctors. I decided to become a doctor so I could overcome this feeling of being uneasy. But medical school was not the answer I was looking for; my studies weren't the answer; the school wasn't the answer; my relationship to others wasn't the answer.

My parents and grandparents and my brother loved me, but I did not feel worthy to receive the love so I had to get the best marks in school (when I didn't have the best marks - when I got less than the best - I came home and cried and my parents did everything to calm me down. They said, "Okay, Walther, we know you are working."). Many kids played; I did not. I learned, not because I wanted to learn, but because I wanted to please my parents and to receive affection. Everyone was proud of me. My brother preferred to play. He had girlfriends. I regret that I didn't have girlfriends. I learned to pay a high price for the love of my parents. I thought I had to pay a high price for the love they were willing to give me free.

Everything that I did was to get others to love me. I

was afraid to lose the contact with others. Later on I was timid. I didn't like myself. I was thinner than I am now and I could never wear shorts. I looked like the stork! I also had acne. At the age of 15 I was supposed to wear glasses but I didn't wear them. When I went through the country I saw wonderful flowers, but they weren't flowers. They were thrown away papers and cigarette boxes!

I suffered very much during the war. I couldn't understand why human beings kill each other or why I should be sent to another country to be a soldier and to fight. During my first month in the German Air Force, I wanted to desert and go to Switzerland, but then a law was passed that said the family of any deserter would be sent to a concentration camp, so I had to go. Every day in the barracks and through the marches I was praying for God to help me because I didn't want to kill. During the three years I was in the Air Force, I never personally killed anyone. I was not in active combat, but as a specialist for parachutes, for instance, and serving in other ways, I helped bombard London and all the other cities, so I participated. I'm not free from guilt.

I was still searching, and I knew that what I was doing was not what I really wanted to do. I thought medicine would be the answer, but it was not.

In 1949 I married. My wife was already a doctor, having studied during the war. She was a beautiful woman, but I was a baby and I was not able to take responsibility for a marriage. When I heard she was pregnant, we were married, because I wanted to do the "right" thing. But I felt as if I were in a cage or a prison. I didn't feel ready yet, even though I was twenty-six years old. I was immature, unable to give the right answer to the situation, unable to respond - I was in a state of ir-response-ability. During this time I thought about an abortion. I was ashamed of these thoughts, because I knew it was wrong, but I thought about it. When I see my daughter, who is now twenty-seven years old, I know it is a crime. But I was just weak, feeble, a little baby. How can a little baby have a baby and be responsible? It is impossible.

My parents and my parents-in-law did everything to help us and I was thrilled when the baby was born, but I felt like an animal in the zoo, restless like a tiger in a cage because he's not in his own world. I made life miserable for my wife. She was much more mature than I was. She tried everything. She understood what is necessary in life, what the first things are, and I always thought of the second ones. I had many good ideas in my head. I wanted to travel and study in foreign countries but I didn't want to accept reality. This gave me trouble and led to severe depression and many attempts at suicide. I know today that my suicidal attempts, fantasies, and ideas were only the expression, the signal for me that I had to change my way of living. Today I understand that suicidal ideas are blessings if you take the right meaning which is that you have to change your life, to get rid of your actual existence and find a new existence. This was very hard to do. It is as hard to do as to commit suicide. I give lectures in my clinic and one of the lectures I give is entitled, "How to commit suicide in the proper way." Most of my guests are there to find out the best way to kill themselves. They find out that I don't have the same meaning for suicide. The way of living in which we cannot cope with reality has to be eliminated - has to be killed to find a new way of living, a new existence. A caterpillar must die to become a butterfly. He never would become a butterfly if he wasn't ready to die. This is the same as we must do and it is hard because you know exactly that when you are still a caterpillar that you are a caterpillar, but when you give up, you never know if you will become a butterfly.

I got a scholarship to study medicine in France, to escape responsibility in my marriage. During my stay in Paris, my wife divorced me. Later on she found someone who was really a mature person who could take on the responsibility of marriage. He also became responsible for my daughter. I could not assume this responsibility.

Because we had too many doctors in Germany, I was

not paid. In 1954, at age thirty, I joined the American Army in Munich and I served for four years as a surgeon. I thought I would emigrate to the United States. During the first month of duty, a sergeant came to my office and said, "You are our new battalion surgeon and I would like to talk to you. Do you know anything about Alcoholics Anonymous?" I said, "Alcoholics Anonymous? No." I thought at first that this was a club where people drink anonymously so they cannot be blamed.

After reading the Twelve Steps, I thought that it was a sect, one of the many sects existing in the United States. Since I wanted to make a living in the United States, I thought I had better become acquainted with this sect. I can't remember the sergeant's name, but today I believe that angels really exist, that they are in the form of human beings. The sergeant asked me how I would treat alcoholics. I said, "That's easy. I learned about that in medical school. They are not fun for a doctor. Just lock them up, observe them, dry them out, and release them. If they have a slip, just lock them up again - and again - and again." He said, "Why don't you come to our meetings and look into our way?" The group had only been meeting since October 1953, and there were only three Germans in this American group, so actually AA did not exist in Germany at that time. I attended closed meetings regularly and they adopted their battalion surgeon. They treated me very gently until one day they mentioned that I should take the cotton out of my ears and put it in my mouth. This was a real touching way to tell me to learn to listen. It was good advice. In the beginning, it hurt me a little bit, but since they were so nice to me I decided to accept it. I was introduced to Al-Anon at this time also. After the AA meeting we would go to a soldier's home and have an Al-Anon meeting there.

I am so grateful to the sergeant because I was allowed to hear all the stories of these men. I learned that they were my own story. I saw that my life and their lives were very similar - with one exception, I did not drink, but I found many ways of being irresponsible. I could identify with them and wanted to belong to their fellowship. I felt miserable when I thought that I did not actually belong because I was not an alcoholic. I did not tell them that I came there because I wanted to be one of them, because I wanted to be accepted, that this was what I was looking for. I found a fellowship where I did not have to hide any more, where I did not have to be strong any more, where I did not have to know everything, where I could admit my weaknesses, my shortcomings and not be judged or condemned but be accepted and even loved, really loved. In the outside world, I thought I had to play a role, many different roles - I had to play a role with my girlfriend, a role as a battalion surgeon, a role with the soldiers, a role when I appeared as a German in a town, a role as a doctor. At AA I was able to feel liberated — free — because no role was required except to be an open human being — to be sincere, and that was all. To have this gift of acceptance was wonderful. When I look back, I did not feel much of a change in myself, but today I can see the Twelve-Step Program experienced in the meetings of Alcoholics Anonymous had a great impact on me. I felt a guidance from God, beginning with the sergeant who told me about AA. I did not feel alone anymore. I felt more secure and that there was a purpose and a meaning in life. Then many years of desert and darkness came. I had many experiences with women because I thought when I found the right woman all of my problems would be solved.

One good part of my story is my meeting my present wife. I was a chief of clinics, with much medical responsibility, but I was hiding my real self behind my white coat, my titles, my cerebral knowledge. Everybody stared at me, everybody believed me, everybody thought that I was a white magician. Underneath this white coat was a little insecure boy who was shy, timid and afraid of many things, especially women. My wife and I were introduced by a friend of mine who belonged to a German-French club which met for better understanding. We fell in love and developed a closer relationship - closer than I wanted at first. I still wanted to run away when I had to be responsible in personal relationships. I loved to take over responsibility as a doctor because there I was safe. But I was not safe in my personal relationships. When my wife told me that she felt blessed, I did not feel blessed at all. I felt dis-ease, miserable. The same thoughts that I had had in 1949 returned. My wife was seventeen years younger that I in age but she was thirty-two years more mature than I at this time. My wife said, "Okay, Walther, you can do what you want to. I am sure I can handle this. I will have the baby. You do what you want to do." I was on the spot! So I decided to at least fake assuming responsibility. I wanted to be a grownup person so I "acted as if." But that was all. We were married and on our wedding night, while my wife was in the bathroom taking a shower, I took three sleeping pills. I had never done this before in my life. When my wife came back, well-dressed and fresh, there was a snoring man. Can you imagine my wife's reaction - her brand-new husband not moving, deadly sleeping and snoring. So my wife wandered around town that night just wondering what she had gotten herself in for. I know now that this was my way of telling my wife that I felt unable to take all the responsibility that was on me, that I didn't know what to do, that I wanted to flee, escape, run away, die or whatever, that I couldn't take it. I awoke in the morning with a terrible headache. It wasn't my wife who had the headache, it was me. We started living together, and I tried more and more to become a grown-up person, with my wife's help.

Through an American member of AA who had been sent by his firm to Western Germany, I heard about a Twelve-Step Program for emotional health in 1967. The first moment I received the address, I wrote. I said to myself, "This must be the fellowship for me. Finally I have found something." I ordered all the periodicals from the beginning. I read all the stories and was able to identify. I said, "These are all my brothers and sisters."

I started a group in the hospital. I waited until my boss was away on vacation because he did not like groups. When he came back, he was really angry with me because I had done that. Later on, he was quite impressed by the group. At the meetings I was faced with the fact that I could not sit there in my white coat, as the chief of clinics of the hospital. I think you all know how difficult it was for me to say the first time, "I'm Walther, and I'm a neurotic." I could only mumble the words. I felt a lot of growth myself and saw much growth among the other members, but when I moved to another town, the old group collapsed because there was no one to support them.

In 1970, at the thirty-fifth birthday of AA in Miami Beach, Florida, we met Marion and some other members of the Twelve-Step Program for emotional health. I was invited there as a guest speaker and I spoke on the subject of AA abroad. I was very much impressed with my first EA meeting in the states, which started the real adventure. This was the actual beginning of my growth which had been prepared many, many years before. I had to come a long way, and I see it was necessary. I made many mistakes. I tried several times to escape the Program. I tried hard, but I could not escape and that is wonderful. I tried to tell myself that this Program might be good for people who are in worse condition than I am, but finally I accepted the Program. Now I can say, along with others, the longer I'm in the Program the newer it appears to me. I am discovering things I have never seen before and the more I take out, the more comes out. I know that it will be a way of life for me for the rest of my life. And today I can accept my life, my past, with all the mistakes I've made and the harm I did to my fellow man. I wish to be able to walk with you, sharing with you all of the richness, fullness, and abundance of life, with the rest of the years that might be given to me.

My mother is seventy-eight and her memory is quite weak. Sometimes she doesn't even know where she is, but recently, while I was walking with her, she said, "Walther,

I have the impression you've found your way in life, your meaning in life." I was so surprised to hear her say that. "You know what you've got to do in life." I said, "Mother, you are right. It took me a hell of a long time to realize this and I know you suffered a lot. I'm very grateful to you and to father for all the patience you had with me." She said, "You know, Walther, I've thought about it and have realized that maybe we did too much for you. You should have done more for yourself." I felt so great. There was a real true understanding of two adult persons. It was wonderful. It did not matter to me whether my mother could find her way around or not or that she didn't know what day it was. We understood each other; I'm very grateful.

Walther

(7)

MY TOOLS FOR SERENITY

It is a very growing and rewarding experience for me
to write and share with you some of my life, how EA works
in my life and how difficult it was to exist before.

There have been many people in my life who have
suffered because of my trouble with my emotions, especially
my family, friends, and work associates. But I'm very thankful that somehow through all the misery in my life, I have
come to know myself and be able to be a little more honest
with myself and others.

As a child, I often heard the comment made to my
dad, "What a shy little boy you have there." As I look back
now, I realize I adapted myself to that image. In school,
I would not get up in front of the class. I withdrew into
myself, unable to go out and meet people. Whenever something came up that I couldn't face, I would react in a shy
manner. I did not realize that I was harming myself nor did
I realize that to be happy, I would have to do the reaching
out myself.

I felt I was beneath the few friends I had. I was
ashamed of my family. We were very poor and I felt everybody else had better circumstances and better living conditions than I.

We didn't have any newspapers to read, so at night we
would sit down at the table, eat, get up and go to bed. If
I was up at 8:30 in the evening doing homework, I was up
late! I was in bed at 8:00 until I was eighteen. I just existed!
There was little sharing or conversation in my home.

After age eighteen, I changed that. I never went to bed

before midnight. I could not stand staying at home. At the time, I did not know why I felt that way nor what was happening to me. I had been restricted so long that when I got out, I went everywhere.

I met a beautiful blond who lived in the city whose home even had indoor plumbing! I don't know where I got the idea, but I told a buddy of mine that I would like to marry that girl. We did get married later.

We made one miserable mess! I had married for a little bit of security and mainly, as I look back now, love. I thought it would get me away from my miseries. My wife had left home for the same reasons.

Things weren't going too well and I started to wonder why we were having all these problems and why she didn't do things differently. She had grown up with much more than I. Why didn't she do things my way? I thought she had everything and yet I was trying to be the boss. Everything was all mixed up, no scheduling, no communication, no nothing. I had not realized that to get along, we had to share.

The security and affection I had gained I lost after our first child was born because all her love and affection went to the child. I felt second best, all alone. This feeling of "aloneness" I kept to myself. As we had more children, I felt less a part of the family so I began working seven days a week.

I would come home, go to bed, get up the next morning and go to work, coming home at ten o'clock at night. No matter how long I worked or how much money I brought home, there never was enough! At least that was the excuse I used. Any time there was a disagreement I would say my piece, walk out the door and go to work, regardless of whether I was scheduled to go or not. As I look back now, I see that I used work as an escape when really I did not want to face what was going on at home.

The marriage got worse and worse and I was steadily going downhill. The only thing I had going for me when my wife decided she would no longer live with me was my occupation where I had worked so hard. I discovered just having a trade was not enough to make me happy.

After some counseling and different things, it was suggested that we try the Twelve-Step Program. It took a year from the time it was suggested before I took my wife so she could get all *her* problems straightened out!

The first meeting brought me something else besides just taking her. I heard people there at the meeting describing problems about themselves that were the same as those that were going on inside of me, that I had never shared with anyone.

I had lived in a world all by myself. I was considered a good guy by most people, somebody who didn't cause too much trouble. But on the inside I was very angry and a resentful human being. Every time I had a conversation with anybody, I would talk with anger and resentment.

As I became acquainted with the Program, I found acceptance and began to share with others just a few things about myself. After I felt I knew the Program, I tried to work it by myself because I couldn't face all those people all the time, but I found that it didn't work, so I would go back and absorb some more until I felt I could work the program alone again.

I would fail. I could not maintain the peace of mind and happiness which the others seemed to have without sharing with the others.

Then a tragic thing happened; my wife had to go into the hospital. My emotions, nerves and everything else were running wild. On the way home from seeing her in the hospital and feeling so low from visiting her there where the conditions weren't really very good but which was all we could afford, I felt so out of it all that I stopped at an EA meeting two or three miles down the road.

I made up my mind that I would give my best to the Twelve-Step Program. During the three years I had gone to the meetings off and on, I had seen the same people coming back and getting help. I felt that if they could get help, maybe I should try harder, as I had nothing to lose at that point in my life. That was when I started working the Twelve-Step Program. I felt relief immediately after I had accepted the Twelve Steps for what they are.

I've done so much negative thinking in my life! I have to reprogram myself to think positively. I used to spend the whole day thinking of how and what people were thinking of me and if I was doing a good enough job. I would think of all the bad things. If the boss wouldn't say good morning, I wondered what was on his mind, what had I done wrong. I used to try to say good morning to everybody and if I didn't get a response I would think they did not like me.

I've gotten rid of quite a few of those negative feelings but I have to keep working at them. I seem to have more positive things going for me now. I try now to accept other people and be as real as I possibly can be at that particular moment. I am not playing the sick games that I used to play although I often find the opportunity to do so.

I have found that I have been afraid to be myself. I felt I wasn't as good as anyone else, and couldn't accept myself. While I was growing up, I thought the others had it better than me when really our growing-up conditions were perhaps very similar.

I couldn't accept my family. My mother was in a mental hospital, my wife was in a mental hospital, my sister was a hospital case and my brother was an alcoholic. Just about everyone around me was a mental case and I was heading that way until I was led to this Program.

As I am working the Program, I am able to change a little bit at a time. To me it's a slow process. Everything is slow for me!!! I can be myself. No longer do I have to put the other guy down to lift myself up, which I often did in the past. Now I feel I can give my opinion and if it isn't accepted, fine, and if it is, good.

I know if there's a problem such as a disagreement with somebody, I have a big part in it. If I can remember this, it keeps me out of a lot of trouble.

I have to decide how I want to deal with the problem: with anger and resentment or with love and acceptance. I've got a long way to go, but at least this is a start.

I have to learn to let go after I've done what I can do, but the most important and biggest thing I have learned through the Program is that I have a choice in whatever comes along. I have a choice to get up and go to work in the morning or I can stay lying in bed as I used to when I was so depressed.

For many years if there was a job for five days a week, it kept me going. If I felt important, I could get up and go to work. Saturday would come along and I would be sick for the whole weekend. Monday morning came along and I'd be raring to go!

The word God has always bothered me. It was at a Twelve-Step Retreat that I heard another member say, "I'm afraid to say that word, God, it tears me apart." This was the same as what was going on inside of me! From that time on I felt comfortable and was able to listen more. One person told the group that he had to have help from another source, a power greater than himself, at first the group, and then God. I was inspired. Since then I have shared this with others and just saying the word has helped me.

I have to come to God each day as I am, if I am to get a deeper understanding of Him. I am learning to have my own concept of how I understand God. I have learned what prayer and meditation are to me mainly through other people. It is a very deep feeling that is hard to describe, but when it comes I know what is happening to me. I can accept it and feel comfortable because I have my Higher Power to share with when there isn't anybody else around. Also, I don't have to improve myself to be accepted by God, I can just be me.

I'm a tradesman in the building business and I like to take the Program and refer to it in that respect. When I first found the Program, I looked at it as a box of brand-new tools that I hadn't used before and that I didn't really know how to use. It is the same as a new person coming on the job who hasn't done this type of work previously. He doesn't know which tool to use. To rip a board, he may pull out a crosscut saw which just doesn't work.

I use just about everything in this box of tools. I use every word that is printed in the yellow pamphlet. I am learning which tool to pull out when I am not feeling good about myself or if I am having a dispute with somebody.

Rebuilding my character is similar to the building business. As I was remodeling a house one day I compared it to the Program. I was upstairs doing something and I found I didn't have a footing down below to support what I was doing, so I had to go down in the basement and build a support for what was going on upstairs. In other words, I had to create a better foundation to build on.

I have to continually do this personal remodeling. Sometimes I hear an idea from someone else. I try it. Sometimes it works for me and sometimes it doesn't.

What I have learned through the Program that works best for me, is that I have to give it away. That is, if I don't share with others, I don't seem to keep it. In order to keep these things, I have to share them with other people, at the meetings, over the phone or face to face.

An important turning point in my life was the first Twelve-Step Retreat I attended. It made me feel so good that I wanted to go back for more. I have gone to just about every retreat that I possibly could since. Every one has been like a two-week vacation for me. Even for one day, I get the lift to try new things in the world and at least get a feeling of some acceptance and the courage to attempt to try things in the outside world.

As I continue to do this I am able to have just a little bit more happiness and serenity for a longer period of time. I am trying to reprogram myself to get rid of the character defects that, with the help of God, I have discovered. I don't have to worry about the fears as they have lessened.

I am trying to achieve warmer relationships with people, and not be as afraid of them as I used to be. I would have hold of the ring and would pull myself up but every time I could see daylight, somebody would come along and step on my fingers and down I would go. This feeling lasted for quite some time while I was trying to work the Program. I don't know when it happened but somewhere along the line, I felt I had come up out of this hole and began seeing daylight all the time.

It's really been great for me to let other members of my family have their problems and let me deal with mine. I don't have to take on their responsibilities; I only share with them and try not to give advice, but give them the benefit of my experience.

There is no way possible for me to attempt to show my appreciation to everybody who has ever been in the Program and to everyone who's going to be in the Program. It saved my life! I believe it will probably help our children to deal with their lives just a little bit better too.

I know if I work the Twelve-Step Program I will continue to be able to grow. I appreciate it so much and have gotten so much help with my difficulties that I want to continue to work it. Nobody else has to, but I want to. I have a reason to live here on earth and to just be a person. Once in awhile I want to be better. I want to be super, that's just natural. With the help of the Program, my life and story do not end here.

Russ

(8)

WEAK NERVES

I had come to the point of complete and utter despair: The fear of insanity, death, or suicide. I had sought professional help for my nervousness, and in a five-year period I was hospitalized three times, had shock treatments, took a hundred different kinds of prescribed drugs, saw a psychiatrist off and on, went to weekly counseling in two different time periods (a year each time), went to marriage counseling, talked periodically with a clergyman, and even took my children for help which they didn't need. When my children started school, I was advised to go back to work because keeping busy was supposed to help. But working wasn't the answer either. I still took myself with me.

Despite all attempts to get help, I had gained no insight into myself or life. I was totally, unbelievably, unaware. I had been looking for the magic word or pill that would make me well and happy. I continued in my despair for two more years. I contemplated suicide. I wanted to die, but was afraid of dying and going to hell. I often told my husband, "I feel as if I am living in hell. It can't be any worse than this." I lived in fear of becoming insane and being committed to an institution. I felt like a failure in every area of my life and thought everyone would be better off if I were dead. I often thought, "My God, if this is what life is all about, I don't want any part of it."

I grew up on a farm, the youngest of twelve children. My life was as normal as anyone's life in a family of that size, but I felt inferior and without acceptance and love from others even though it might have been there. I tried hard to be like those I respected and looked up to, for I thought this imitation would win me acceptance. My feelings of not measuring up were intensified by my being overweight and wearing thick glasses. Because I was sensitive and would over-react, I was a prime target for much teasing and nick-names which I interpreted as rejection of me. I was very frightened about going to school. I didn't know one person in my class and didn't want to get to know anyone. I never learned to like school.

When I was eleven, my father died suddenly of a heart attack. It was a terrible shock and for a long time I prayed that God would send my father back. Shortly after my father's death, my mother was hospitalized with a nervous breakdown. I felt alone and afraid and talked to no one. I thought God was the cause of all this and my fear of Him increased. I felt he was keeping records of everything I did wrong and I would have to make up for my wrongs with suffering and acts of penance.

I began to feel that it was dumb and stupid to be afraid and I started to deny some of my feelings. I was certain that showing emotion would bring ridicule. In school I picked up the idea that feelings of anger, jealousy, hate, envy, and revenge were bad feelings and sinful. I had a surplus of these feelings, and was certain God would not love me because He only loved those who were good. As a result, I started more and more to use the defense of denial. I wanted to be good, virtuous, and above moral reproach. I developed a rigid morality along with the fear of showing my true feelings because I wanted acceptance from God and everyone else.

High school did nothing to improve my self worth. I really hated it. Except for a handful of friends, I was afraid of reaching out to make new relationships. I put the responsibility on the other person to make the initial move of friendliness. I depended on the behavior of others for my own happiness.

As soon as I turned sixteen I found a job and proceeded to buy clothes with every penny I made. I thought having nice clothes would give me a sense of security. I also lost some weight, but neither the nice clothes nor the trimmer me gave me what I was looking for. Because I had such bad feelings about my thick glasses, at eighteen I invested in my first pair of contact lenses. I liked my lenses, but they didn't change my inner feelings about myself.

During my formative years, I picked up negative, unhealthy attitudes about my sexuality and was not able to accept my sexual feelings. This caused me much guilt and depression which I couldn't talk to anyone about.

I thought the answer to my problems would be to get married and have a family, so, at the age of twenty, after two and a half years of a stormy courtship, I married. But instead of marriage being the answer, I felt more insecure than ever. I had no sense of commitment or responsibility in the relationship and discovered years later I was really looking for a daddy. I had two children very close together and was overwhelmed. I tried to cover up the inadequacy I felt inside by keeping my house and children perfect.

When my youngest was five months old, the bottom fell out of my life. I went to my obstetrician crying, and he sent me to a psychiatrist who prescribed pills. The pills didn't help and I became more and more depressed. I cried and cried, but didn't know why. I was unable to handle the smallest responsibility and was hospitalized with my first nervous breakdown. I was given shock treatments and drugs. I have no recollection of what my life was like for those weeks in the hospital and the months that followed. All I remember is that it was extremely hard for me to handle things when I got back home. I continued taking many prescribed drugs and was going to a counselor where we talked about surface things only. I was hoping some pill would cure my "weak nerves" or God would work some miracle in my life so I would be well.

As time went on and my mind became a little clearer, I thought, "God, why did you give me weak nerves?" I began to feel fearful, guilty, and scrupulous. I felt that God was punishing me by denying me the things I desperately needed. I felt that I would possibly end up in an institution because nerves were hereditary. My only hope was that God would work a miracle. I began to pray like I had never prayed before.

As the months went by, I existed with weekly visits to a counselor and prescription drugs. But my symptoms continued — unhappiness, nervousness, worrying, remorse, fatigue, boredom, insomnia, suicidal thoughts, loneliness, even in a crowd, abnormal fears, and extreme guilt. I became more and more compulsive, checking and counting everything in my house. I really thought I was going crazy.

Fear and anxiety were strong on the night our house was hit by a series of three tornadoes. My thoughts returned to my failures and mistakes. I thought of how hard I had been on my husband and children. My prayer for our safety was, "God, I'll try to do better. Please let us live." The night passed into morning. The glass was blown out of the windows so they had to be boarded up, and the electricity was out for several days. It was like living in a dungeon. I was afraid of its happening again. I had just finished spring housecleaning and had to face doing it all over again. I couldn't stand for anything to be out of order as this was the only area in which I felt any worth.

I became depressed and anxious and was hospitalized again. I worried what my neighbors and relatives would think. I felt so ashamed. I didn't want anyone to know. But when I unexpectedly received some flowers from a group of neighbors, I felt grateful for their acceptance of me.

After an uneventful stay in the hospital, I was released. My medications were cut in half and I suffered severe withdrawal symptoms. I thought surely I was going crazy and for three days and two nights lived in the worst panic I had ever felt before or since. I still had to face what I had tried to escape from — the mess in my house and the mess inside of me.

Periodically the panicky feeling would recur. I could

not rationalize away my obsessive thoughts like I had been able to do before. I wanted to be patient, kind, and loving, but the more I tried to control my behavior, the more out of control I seemed to be. I couldn't seem to help myself.

At times I would run to a clergyman looking for reassurance. At other times I would pace the floor in the middle of the night, sure I was dying or going insane. I was extremely frightened of death in those moments that seemed to last forever. When I felt depressed I wished I could die. When I felt anxious I was afraid I was going to die. This was my existence for another year and a half.

Severe headaches that nothing would help once again sent me to the hospital. I was sure there was something physically wrong. They ran every conceivable test and found nothing. I greeted this news with relief because I was afraid of being cut into, but I was disappointed that whatever was wrong with me could not be simply removed.

After reading a pamphlet on the will of God and suffering, I decided that it was God's will for me to be sick, so I tried to be a "martyr" and accept it. I went home from the hospital with a great deal of medication. I was absolutely useless with all the pills so I proceeded to cut down gradually on the dosage.

Fearing hospitalization again, I once more went in search of help. Eight months before, I had heard two members of a Twelve-Step Program for people with emotional problems being interviewed on the radio. At the time, I did not identify with those people because my problem was my "weak nerves." But somewhere in the back of my mind the thought stayed. I asked my psychiatrist about the group and he encouraged me to try it.

I was skeptical, but I finally attended my first meeting. At that meeting someone said, "Come for three months and if you don't like what you have received, we'll gladly refund your misery." What did I have to lose? At first I thought someone was going to do something for me, but I soon learned that I was going to have to take some positive action. Getting to meetings became my top priority.

I began to find hope and realized for the first time in my life that I wasn't some oddball after all. I wasn't alone.

After about two months of meetings, I was more excited about what I had found in this Program than about anything that had ever happened in my life. At first I was frightened when people talked openly about their feelings, but I began to realize that in being honest about their thoughts and feelings, they were able to rid themselves of the painful symptoms that were yet overwhelming me. It was hard to admit to the feelings that caused my nervousness — self-pity, resentment, anger. But I learned that no matter how justified I might feel for having these feelings, they are the ones that destroy me if I don't face them and let them go. With the insight and courage that I gained through the Program, I was able to look back at my life. Hurt has to be looked at to be healed.

As I continued to go to weekly meetings, I learned this hell I was living was self-made because I could not or would not accept reality. I learned hell was actually being self-centered, living in my own little world all alone, and not the fire and brimstone I was taught as a child. I learned about the Serenity Prayer which in brief means either I accept a situation or I change it. If I don't do either, I will develop another neurosis.

To get well was going to take time and patience. I found it very easy to admit I was "powerless" because I remembered all my own attempts to try to change myself that had only made me sicker. I had to give up control of my life and admit I wasn't self-sufficient. I learned to be honest about my feelings. It was a great relief to find my thoughts and feelings were not any different from those of any other human being. I had been afraid that if I acknowledged my thoughts and feelings I would automatically act on them, but I learned that recognizing and facing a feeling means I will have the choice to act or not act on it. Denial of my feelings gives *them* control over *me*.

I also had to learn to stop blaming either myself or others. I was told that it didn't matter why or how I got sick, but whether I was willing to do something about it today. The responsibility of getting well depended on me. Others would be there for my support. I had to make the effort with the help of a Higher Power, God as I understood Him.

For the first time in my life I had to face the fact that it was my choice to stay sick or get well. I was frightened that maybe I couldn't make it and yet relieved that it was inside of me to make this effort. If it was outside of me, as I had previously thought, then I would be helpless to change. It was very frightening to think about looking at myself, but I had to talk about all my feelings, no matter how embarrassing or frightening, before I could begin to accept them. Without acceptance there could be no healing.

My insight came slowly. Through people, books, and times of quiet I began to lose my fears of what I would find in myself next. I learned that God did not cause the negative things to happen in my life. He was not responsible for my illness, but allowed it through giving me free will to make my own choices.

As I overcame my pride and fear of rejection, I was able to reach out to other people and realize how God works through them. The encouragement and acceptance I found from people was the most freeing thing I have ever experienced. I took my first Fifth Step and lost my fear of clergymen. I found they were not shocked by what I had to say. Their remarks were, "Welcome to the human race." I experienced for the first time the feeling that God must really love me to have sent these loving, accepting people into my life.

I used to think I had humility when I continually ran myself down by saying I was no good. I didn't think of myself as a proud, egotistical person. But today I see a lot of pride — not accepting myself as I am because I think I am supposed to be great. I also learned to deal with guilt, constantly thinking, "I really should have done better." I had to learn to accept that I had done the best

I could at the time and must continue doing what I can today. Once I could accept that God forgave me for my mistakes, I had to learn to forgive myself or I would be putting
myself above God. I came to understand a little of the
mercy and forgiveness of this Power greater than myself.

In the early years of the Program, because I was so
idealistic, I became easily discouraged, but I hung on because I certainly didn't want to go to the hospital again.
I also was able to gain strength from the people who gave me
encouragement and believed in me. I started to recognize
progress. My symptoms started to fall away and I began to
see some good in myself. The pride that had destroyed me
before now became my asset for I was too proud to give
up. When things seemed too painful or tough, I could look
back to where I had been, and the thought of going back
there put me on the right track again.

My inner growth is reflected outwardly in the new
experiences I will venture into, knowing these experiences
will increase my faith in a loving God. One experience I am
grateful for is the attainment of my driver's license. Because
of my fear of driving, I had continually renewed my driver's
permit for sixteen years. One fall morning I took my
driver's test and passed. One of the first places I drove to,
I was carrying the message of EA to a group of professional
people. It was the first snowfall of the season and very
slippery, but I was not going to be a seasonal driver. A
friend later teased me about having driven in the first snow
storm with, "You were too dumb to know the difference."
But I had faced my fears. Growth only comes when I am
willing to take a risk.

With my new independence I find that by not being
afraid to depend on others, I can stand more on my own
feet. I need people, but my need for people is much health-
ier now. I am appreciating the love of my family and friends
and I am slowly learning to love and accept myself and others.

The psychiatrist who was treating me when I was so
ill has expressed his amazement at the fantastic recovery I
have made. He has publically endorsed EA and has the

program available for his patients when they are in the hospital. A clergyman who I used to run to often, commented to a friend of mine, "I wouldn't have given two bits that she would make it." After a couple years in EA, I was invited by him to talk with some seminary students about EA. This past winter I had occasion to sit down with the person I had taken my first Fifth Step with. During the conversation he remarked to me, "You have come a long way, baby." This feedback from people who knew me when I was the sickest has been very rewarding, but I owe it all to EA.

One night when I had been in the Program for about a year, my eight-year-old son called me into his room and said, "Mom, you have really changed." I said, "In what way?" He answered, "You're more loving."

The most recent experiences the program has helped me to deal with are the death of my mother, my mother-in-law, and my father-in-law. Death earlier was my greatest fear. Before my mother died, I was able to come to understand her and to love her. It was a very hard relationship for me to handle because I was so much like her, but through EA I had become able to be honest with her, and this helped. My father-in-law died a painful death from cancer. Until his illness we were uncomfortable around each other and didn't have much of a relationship. We had some beautiful talks those last eight months about life and death. My mother-in-law had been in good health and while we were expecting my father-in-law to die, she died suddenly of a heart attack just about five weeks before he died. When his children went to the cancer home to tell him of her death, after his initial shock, he said, "How will Pat take this?" When my husband told me this, I cried because it touched me so deeply. Good can come out of tragedy if only I will look for it.

There is still more pain in my life these days, as one of my teenagers is having to go through things the hard way to come to terms with reality in his life. I can't save him or fix him up, even with all the great things I've learned, nor do I have the right to.

There are many other such experiences that I have had in these past eight years. Today I wouldn't trade all the struggles, pains, joys, and growth experiences for anything because they are what have brought me to where I am.

The miracle I prayed for so long in my life has happened but not in the way I expected. I had to want to change enough to discipline myself and to put at least as much effort into getting well as I put into being sick. I have not arrived. Today I am still in this process of discovering who I am and what I believe in. Sometimes my self-destructive patterns try to reassert themselves, but I am now aware. My negative attitudes of thirty years are in my subconscious, always ready to rear their ugly head, but I can choose to say no to this self-defeat and venture out to meet a new challenge.

A whole new world has opened to me since finding EA. I owe my existence to this new way of life where I found a God who loves me, imperfect as I am, and touches me through people. The most crucial thing I found in the fellowship of EA is friends who have been through similar experiences, who don't want to blame and find excuses for their illness any longer, but who want to face themselves honestly and see the part they have played in their problems.

I have learned that shock treatments and pills are only temporary relief. All they do is treat the symptoms. I have learned too that weak nerves, or nervousness, or whatever you want to call it, is just a symptom of emotional illness.

I would have never believed that the denial or repression of my emotions could have caused me the physical, mental, emotional, and spiritual pain I experienced if I hadn't been through this hell myself.

In the past eight years I have changed from a person feeling totally worthless, helpless, inferior, and full of symptoms, to a person whose life has found purpose and meaning far beyond what I could have imagined. I have gratitude and love in my heart for those people who have helped me to start to discover me — a person with worth and potential no one could have convinced me of before I found EA.

Pat

(9)

I FELT LIKE A DUMB BLONDE

First of all I want to tell you I have never been hospitalized, been to a psychiatrist, or taken a pill, but I am a neurotic because I have difficulties dealing with the reality of the here and now.

I have been aware of this Program for about eleven years. I have been attending meetings for about eight years. My awareness of the Program came when my husband began attending meetings. I noticed a change in him and the tension in the house was not as great. The reason for this, I now realize, was that he was learning to take responsibility for his behavior and his own feelings. I began reading the literature and attended a couple of open meetings and decided I could use the Program, too. I had the Just For Today's taped on my cupboard long before I attended meetings. My main reason for starting the Program was that I wanted to become a good mother. I felt completely inadequate as a mother, which I will go into later.

I will start by telling you a little about myself and my family background. I was born and raised on a farm in southern Minnesota. Being the youngest of six children, I was pampered by my sisters and brothers, but they also took their frustrations out on me.

My parents had immigrated to this country from Europe. They did not speak English very well. We were poor; others in the community seemed to have more material things than we did. Somehow I grew up with the feeling that being a farmer and being poor were synonymous with being stupid. During my grade school years I fluctuated between feeling inferior and seeing my friends have more material things than I had, and feeling superior because in the one-room school I went to I did very well scholastically. There was also one family I admired which showed affection for one another quite freely. In my family I was told this was silly. But I was always fascinated by their affection for one another.

When I was in ninth grade we were bussed to town for high school. This was a traumatic experience for me. In my small country school I could be on top, but in a large school I felt I could not be, so I didn't even try. I spent four miserable years never opening a book, feeling very inadequate, lonely, and frustrated. I thought that when I got off this lonely farm and graduated from high school, I would be happy. In fact, for all of my life my happiness was in the future.

Well, I graduated from high school and moved to Minneapolis to work. Minneapolis was a good place to hide and in a way I did hide. I met people at work and through my sisters, but I never let anyone really know me. I dealt with people in a superficial way. I was happy and friendly, and always a pleaser to the point of trying to be the kind of person I thought they wanted me to be. This went on until I really didn't know who I was or what I thought. I was always wearing a mask. I was afraid to really let anyone know me, afraid of rejection, and letting them discover I was not perfect.

As I said before, my happiness was always in the future. I thought when I got married I would be happy. I thought my husband would make me feel loved and worthwhile. But unfortunately for me, he was only a human being with his own insecurities. The responsibilities and demands of marriage really made me feel inadequate. Now I realize the one person who can make me happy and secure is me.

After a couple of years we had two children, a girl and a year later a boy. Then my problems really began. I resented those babies because I felt tied down. I felt completely responsible for their physical and emotional well-being. If they caught a cold it was my fault. When they had fears or problems with their peers it was my fault. Needless to say there were many problems, both physical and emotional, in their growing up and I always felt guilt and self-hate. I became very defensive. I never stopped to enjoy my children as human beings.

I started attending EA meetings when they were in their early teens, which is the best thing that ever happened to me. I remember what a revelation those first meetings were. Here were people from all walks of life sitting down and telling others how they really felt. And what a surprise — they had the same lonely, strange feelings I had. I thought I was so unique and I had never told anyone of these feelings, but best of all, here were people saying these feelings are okay, and they were doing something about them with the help of the Program.

The Program contains the tools to my happiness and security. The first thing that hit home with me was that I wasn't all that important to my children. Also, that I was not God; that there is an Infinite Being who has something to do with our lives if we let Him. These children were not mine to control; they had a right to grow up and make their own decisions and mistakes. What a relief! I had a responsibility to them, but not for their behavior.

So I quit worrying about being a good mother and began concentrating on myself. I had to look within and find out what I was really feeling. I had to look behind intolerance, jealousy, resentment, deceit, and look at all my fears. For me this was always painful. Some of it was buried pretty deep and I didn't like what I saw. The more I ran away, the lower my self-esteem became. I have found it always goes back to what I think of myself. I'm very idealistic and thought I should be very special, so I have been running away from the real me. I had to stop running and accept that I feel like a "dumb-blonde farmer." I once heard someone say, if you know you're crazy, you're not. Then I quit running around doing stupid things like trying to be someone I was not. There is so much peace of mind in acceptance for me, I wonder why I fight it so much because it frees me to be the real me, which isn't dumb at all.

After eight years in the Program I still find life is not a bowl of cherries, but it is something I can cope with, one day at a time. Recently we had two deaths in the family within a month. One was my brother, who suffered from a long and painful battle with cancer. I was with him the afternoon he died. I was amazed by the peace and serenity I felt with the thought of death. In the past I would have run from this situation. A couple of weeks later my brother-in-law died of a heart attack, and after the funeral I stayed behind with my sister for a few days, something I never would have been able to do before because I would have felt I had to take her grief away. Now I realize that all I can do for another person is to listen and be there.

My children are now twenty-one and twenty-two years old and will be leaving home soon. This may sound strange to some of you, but I'm looking forward to their leaving. I can let them go without feeling any guilt. Sure I made plenty of mistakes, but I now realize that I'm only a human being and that's okay. I did the best I could. I can let them go to be free and make their own mistakes. This is the greatest gift I believe I can give them.

I'm having problems right now not knowing what I want to do with the rest of my life. I ask myself: Do I want a job or don't I? Could I support myself or couldn't I? I find myself wanting to control my husband. I feel he works too hard, but my only peace of mind is in letting go. All of these are the problems I'm dealing with today, but the answers will come because I have people in my groups to talk to. I have the Twelve-Step Program and my Higher Power. How do I know this? Because it has worked in the past if I just live one day at a time.

Helen

(10)

WORKAHOLIC

My name is LeRoy and I am powerless over my emotions and I am also a workaholic.

My story began on a farm in west central Minnesota where I lived with my father, mother, brother, and four sisters. Because I was the oldest, I became a controller and manipulator at a very young age. I also became a person who tried more and more to gain acceptance and love from my peers and everyone else around me by excelling at everything I did. I never was satisfied with being second in anything I did. I had to be number one. This continued through high school and later when I was on my own. I didn't have many friends as the only friends I accepted were people I could overrule or dominate.

About two years after I graduated from high school I got married to a girl I had been dating for about a year. It seemed the thing to do — to get married because everyone else was doing it. We had our arguments when dating and after we got married. Being a very domineering and controlling person, I tried to manage my wife's life. My wife wouldn't or couldn't be controlled and manipulated. As a result we fought continuously.

My wife became pregnant right after we were married. Twin girls were born. This only added to our problems because now our financial burdens became greater and I couldn't do the best on my job because I was continually tired from all the fighting. The only reason we stayed together at this time was because of our strong upbringing and the way people in our lives looked at divorce. It was just out of the question. We were going to resolve this marriage problem, even if it was the last thing we did and it almost was. As the years went by we continued to fight.

I tried many different types of jobs to find one that I could really like. These jobs were working on farms, and eventually I got a job working for the University of Minnesota Experiment Station. I started to go to college part-time and eventually went full-time. At this time my wife was working, we had the two children, and I was going to school full-time and working part-time. This is when we were having the worst problems with our marriage, probably because of the tremendous pressures we were putting on ourselves. After about a year and a half, I decided to leave school and go into sales full-time (I had been in sales part-time while going to school). This decision was very hard on my wife because she had built up a fantasy that I would land a big job and be very successful when I graduated. Then our problems became worse, and after seven years of marriage we were at a point where we either were not speaking or we were in a knock-down terrible word battle with each other.

We finally decided that we had to do something so we went to a psychologist, to pastors, to a marriage counselor, and to friends. None of these people seemed to have a solution. We expected them to find some magic formula for solving our problems but it didn't happen. One night we were still arguing at three a.m. Our pastor-marriage counselor had given us his home telephone number. I called him and asked him what we could do because nothing seemed to work. The next time we saw him I felt God was taking over and a miracle was happening. We were in his office and he mentioned he had received a professional packet from a Twelve-Step Program for people with emotional problems — Emotions Anonymous. He gave us the pamphlet and suggested we check it out as he didn't know much about it.

We called the number and went to our first EA meeting. All I remember at that meeting is that I was loved and accepted by these people and I wanted more. After the first meeting I made a big mistake and forced a discussion with my wife. In the ensuing argument she became totally turned off from the Program. She didn't start going to meetings for a year and then only because I was finally able to let go of her was she able to go by herself, for herself. Our marriage slowly began to improve. This I feel was because at my first meetings I learned that the only person I could change was myself. When I stopped trying to change my wife, we didn't have as many fights.

The first major thing that happened to me, and it happened gradually, was that I learned to love and be loved. When I joined EA I was like a stone. The only person who concerned me was myself. When the twins were born I was told by society that it was supposed to be a big thing. Well, for me it didn't mean anything; in fact, if I could have, I wouldn't even have gone to the hospital when they were born. I can remember being resentful that my wife didn't have the girls early in the evening so I wouldn't have to miss any work!

This is where I have to explain how I saw I am powerless over being a workaholic. To me a definition of a workaholic is a person who lets work be his God. I let work control me in every way. I don't know if it was because I had a poor image of myself and being successful in my work was a way to build myself up, or if it was because of something else. But the fact is, I let my work control me.

In EA at that time I was slowly getting a better image of myself and was acquiring more self-worth. In other words, I was learning how to love myself. I was an average salesman, but by putting all my energy into my job, I became fairly successful. The problem was that I was spending all my time working and very little time with anything else, including my wife, my family, or myself.

After about three years I was promoted to an assistant manager and shortly after that promoted to a manager. My workaholic tendencies really took over then and I was going to be successful or else. I worked day and night and I was very seldom home. I traveled a lot and held many meetings for the people I was managing. At the same time I was feeling increased pressure from above me to be more successful so I could be promoted again. I was so hard on myself that I am sure now that either I would have had an emotional breakdown or a physical breakdown. It was just a matter of time. I was feeling all kinds of symptoms such as soreness in my neck, tightness in my throat, and chest pains. I was eating Tums by the bottle and my stomach was in a continuous turmoil. There was never a halfway point for me. I was either completely in it or completely out of it.

I had been reading a book and I could identify with a lot of things the author said about himself. One thing that I had latched onto was "Go and do the things where your bones feel the most comfortable." With the help of going to many EA meetings and talking to many people, meditating by myself, and going through turmoil, I decided to resign. I got a job as a maintenance mechanic. I took this job because I decided to let the job, with God's help, control me. I forced myself not to work any more overtime than I had to.

One problem with me to this day is that I have to learn to adjust to not being number one all of the time, and also I have to find constructive things to do with my free time. I was working sixty or more hours a week before and now I am working forty hours a week. I found that I had to get away from my family to some extent because this was too big a change for them and for me.

I have found a temporary alternative to this problem — EA. I enjoy working in the EA office and have been spending some of my extra time there. I am gradually able to spend more time at home and hopefully, with the help of my many EA friends, I will be able to adjust better as time goes on, and be able to spend more time with my family.

From thinking and meditating on my job situation, I feel now that I have an addiction to money as an alcoholic has for alcohol, and the only way to satisfy this addiction for money is by being a workaholic. It is not wrong to want money because it is a very necessary thing in my life. But it is wrong when the urge to make money is so strong that it controls every aspect of my life. In essence, it was my God.

I am much happier with the way I am living my life now and feel this is due to working the Program to the best of my ability. With the help of God I am going where "my bones feel the most comfortable."

When I came to the Program I used the group as my Higher Power. Because I had no concept of God, I felt that the group knew more about life or the Program than I did so they could be my Higher Power. I felt there was more to it than that and I needed a more personal relationship with my Higher Power, so I continued to search. I couldn't understand God so I ignored Him. I took a Fifth Step on the Third Step because I had so much trouble working at it. I continued to search and struggle. Then after going to a very touching and meaningful church service, I was driving down the road in my car by myself and I simply exploded. I bawled my head off. At that time I turned my will and life over to God, as I understood Him. There was no struggle; it just happened. I was at a point in my life where I had struggled enough and I let go and let God come into my life. This was the most complete Third Step I've taken. Now I continue to work at getting a more meaningful, personal, and closer relationship with my God. By working the Twelve Steps to the best of my ability, I feel this is happening.

As I go through life I will continue to have my ups and downs. They won't be as extreme, and maybe when I am trying to do everything myself I will be able to "Let go and let God" much faster.

I have found many friends in EA and my whole life is built around these friends. The longer I am in the Program, I find people who I especially identify with and these people are the ones I become closest to. In discussing this with one of my friends, we came to a mutual agreement as to why. We are both extreme workaholics and can learn from each other's growth in doing something about it. There are many other people who I can really identify with and these are the people who I seek out and learn from. This is one of the ways the Program works.

My marriage still has its ups and downs but it is no longer a destructive marriage where we are continually trying to destroy each other. It is a marriage where we are trying to build each other up and we aren't playing the destructive games we were once playing. In fact, we have been married for about fifteen years and we both agree that we feel we only have been married for the eight years we have been in the Program.

I have made great progress in this Program in all areas of my life. I plan to continue to work on these Twelve Steps the rest of my life as I am far from where I would like to be. I will always have something to work on.

In these days of the rat race, as I call it, I need something like this to keep me on the right track so I can live a more serene and happy life.

LeRoy

(11)

MY LIFE WILL BE GREAT WHEN . . .

I was raised in a small rural community, the younger of two children. I learned at a very young age that I could usually get my own way if I was persistent. I think my folks got tired of my pleadings and gave in.

Somehow I had grown up with the idea that every little girl grew up, married, and existed for her family as a wife and mother. My mother helped my father with his business, but I was going to be the perfect type of woman and be the model woman, wife, and mother.

At seventeen I met this wonderful man and at eighteen I married him. He was a farmer and not nearly sophisticated enough for me, but I told myself I would change him to suit me.

Our marriage was rocky from the beginning. I was used to getting my own way and all of a sudden I couldn't get it. I didn't have the money to buy all of the material things that had always been so important to me. I felt trapped and when the argument got rough one time, I got into the car ready to go back home to Mom and Dad, but I was pregnant so I turned around and went back into the house because I didn't want to go through that without my husband.

Nine months after our wedding we had identical twins. I didn't know what to do with one baby, much less two, and I was frightened. Somehow I managed. I remember thinking at that time that because I had been fulfilled so early in my life, perhaps I would die early.

After we'd been married a couple of years, we moved

closer to a metropolitan area and my husband began working for the University. This was my opportunity to improve him. I talked him into taking a class or two and he enjoyed it. If I could convince him to get his degree, he would be successful like a president of a corporation or something, and my life would be fulfilled because I had a very successful husband and everyone *knows* that behind every successful man is a really good wife.

We decided I should go to work so that if he wanted to go to school full time, he would be able to. About a year later we made that decision and packed up and moved to the University. He went to school two years and things were tight, but we were happy. I was living in the future so it didn't bother me to do without things for now. After a couple years, he was having trouble with the physical sciences required for his major and to change majors he would lose a lot of credits. He decided to quit. The bottom fell out of my world. I felt he would be a failure for certain.

I had lost a lot of weight after the girls were born, and while we were in student housing I started to put on a few pounds. I went to the doctor and he gave me diet pills — amphetamines. I felt terrific. I could work all day, work all night at home, go to bed late, get up and pop a pill and I was off again. This lasted several months, and when I ran out of pills about six months later, I crashed. Neither my doctor nor I realized what had happened. He had also treated me for some minor infections along the way. I was getting depressed, I was tired all the time, and I had a low-grade temperature constantly. I finally went into the hospital for some tests, and my biggest fear was that they wouldn't find anything wrong with me and would tell me it was a mental condition. They did find something wrong — that my kidneys were formed differently and infected — but certainly nothing that would be causing my depression.

The depression kept on and I sank lower and lower. I experienced a real identity conflict. I didn't know who

I was, why I was here, or where I was going. Everything I saw was negative. I had the most beautiful picture on my living room wall, and I couldn't see the beauty of it. The colors were all wrong, the balance was off. The depression kept on and I sank deeper. I wanted to know why things were happening to me, and the more I searched for the whys, the more in circles I went and the deeper I sank into depression. I tried tranquilizers but they didn't help me. I was on anti-depressants for several months, but they were a temporary solution. I needed to find the reasons for my feelings, or something I could work with.

I'd lost all contact with God. If there was a God, why would He torture me this way? I felt so all alone, that no person cared for me, and that everyone in my family would be better off without me. I finally reached a point that if I had to go through life feeling the way I felt, I didn't want to live. I contemplated suicide several times and came very close a couple of times. I had some sleeping pills I carried in my purse at all times so that if I ever couldn't stand it any longer, I could cop out. It was a real sense of security to have the pills with me. It was the most frightening experience I have ever gone through.

My husband and I weren't getting along. We couldn't communicate and would play sick games. I knew that if we started to argue and I couldn't stand it any longer, I need only shut him out of my mind, clam up and not talk to him at all. It would drive him to fits of anger. In my sick mind I must have enjoyed seeing him explode. I suppose it justified some of my depression because I was feeling so sorry for myself and I had every reason, being as miserable as I was. We were very close to divorce.

I tried many ways to find the reasons for experiencing this hell on earth. I tried talking to a pastor, marriage counselor, and psychologist, as well as friends. I went through testing and the psychologist told me I was depressed. This was no earth-shattering news — I already knew that. I expected him to lay all of my problems on a silver platter and tell me what I could do to become happy. My expectations of him were so unrealistic, and I couldn't or wouldn't dig into myself for the answers that could only come from within me. Of course, he couldn't help me. My husband and I couldn't communicate, so our marriage counselor couldn't get through to us. He had heard of a Twelve-Step Program for people with emotional problems, and we decided we had nothing to lose by trying it. We went to our first meeting and I was surprised to see all of the normal-looking people sitting around the table admitting they had emotional problems or that they were neurotics. I had expected to see a bunch of nuts crawling the walls.

My husband originally came to see if there was anything he could do to help me with my problem because the psychologist's testing revealed it was all my problem. The tests showed my husband was happy and well-adjusted. He also discovered he had a few problems. As in the past, my husband tried to force the Program on me. I rebelled against him as usual, and decided that I wanted no part of this Program. Also, I wasn't ready to face the honesty that was required in looking at myself.

I noticed my husband gradually began to change. He was going to a lot of meetings and he had a lot of friends. He didn't play the sick games with me anymore and he quit trying to change me. I realized he was feeling better about himself and I was still sitting there and was miserable. Finally I decided to go to a meeting by myself, for myself. From that point on I surrendered and began working the Program.

Today I'm grateful for the depression and all the suffering I had to go through. I probably could not have given myself to this Program and become totally honest with myself if I hadn't been in a crisis situation.

I'm grateful for what the Program has taught me. First of all, I'm a person, and I had to develop a sense of confidence in myself. When I took my first honest inventory in Step Four of the Program, I found out for the first time that I could look at myself honestly, without rationalizing. This was one of the most difficult Steps for me to under-

take. It was a Step of real growth. I found mostly negative things and only a few positives. After being in the
Program for several years, that list of positives has grown
tremendously.

We had put off adopting a baby during my husband's
student years. Our baby himself didn't make me happy,
but he's brought much joy into our lives. He's an inter-
racial child and he'll experience prejudice growing up in our
society. We feel through the Program we're prepared to guide
him and we certainly love him. He's added so much to our
lives.

I didn't have any self-esteem; I had only my husband's.
I learned that my sense of self-confidence had to come from
within myself. Instead of depending on my husband for his
success, I decided I really wanted a degree and I meditated
a lot on it. I'd earned some credits while my husband was
in school, and now with my job, three children, and a
husband who helped a lot, I was able to get that degree.
I didn't do it alone. My Higher Power enabled me to do
it because it obviously was His will for me. There could
have been so many obstacles, but everything worked out.
I had to learn to make plans but not to plan the results.
Somehow everything turned out beautifully.

I have learned that I count. I can do things for myself and it's not always selfish. It is simply healthy. I
can't control another person, nor do I have the right to do
so. In turn, I don't have to let another person control me.

I have found a concept of a Higher Power that I hadn't
found before the Program. Although I grew up with a for-
mal religion, I had a fearful concept of God, and He was a
punishing God. He was keeping score of my wrongs and
someday I'd have to account for them and I certainly would
not measure up. Through the Program, and even more so
the people in the Program, I have come to know a loving
God. I feel that my Higher Power has guided me to places
where I'll grow, whether this be church or community. At
the present I'm very comfortable in a church where I'm
motivated to read, study, and pray. This is God working

through people, whether it be people in the Program or people in the church. It is not being religious - it is being spiritual — which the Program has taught me.

Our marriage has improved dramatically. It is now one where we are able to love and support each other instead of playing sick games and destroying each other. It is constructive rather than destructive. We still have our arguments, but our arguments now get resolved.

I have learned that my emotions aren't bad. I don't have to suppress my tears, joy, and kisses as I was taught in my Norwegian upbringing. In my childhood I had been extremely close to my mother and I felt she compensated for the lack of love from my father. We seldom mentioned the word "love," and we did not kiss or embrace as a lot of families did. I attributed this to our Norwegian culture.

My father had a nervous breakdown when I was born, and somehow I never felt love from him the way my sister seemed to receive it. He watched me go through my depression and tried to talk about some positive things, but I could not respond to him. After I was in the Program awhile, I began to understand and identify with some of his character traits and often desired to talk to him about "us," but I always put it off until the next time I saw him. In many ways we were very much alike. I told myself that some day we'd have a good talk. That day never came. I was called home one Sunday because my father was critically ill in the hospital. He had asthma and emphysema and he was experiencing difficulty with one collapsed lung and was on oxygen. I knew I couldn't burden him with anything heavy, but he allowed me to embrace him. I told him tearfully how much he meant to me and how much I loved him. He told me the feeling was mutual. He died two days later. Years later I was told of the environment in which he was brought up, of his alcoholic father, and of several other shattering events in his younger years. I no longer remember his lack of love for me, but I remember the good times we did have and his positive traits.

It's okay to be me. I don't have to fit a mold or pattern. My husband complained early in our marriage that the house was too perfect; he felt uncomfortable because he might mess something. Today I'm busy with work, activities, the kids, and some class (I'm usually involved in some educational activity because it stimulates my mind). He shakes his head and starts to help pick up the clutter. That's okay too.

With my career I was concerned at one point that I was spending too little time with my children. A friend in the Program pointed out to me that the quality of time I spend with my children is much more important than the quantity. I was a terrible mother at times when I was at home and unhappy. Now my children know they are loved and are always clothed and fed. It's first things first, and I always try to spend some time each day talking with each one about his or her day and any problems or things they want to share with me. It's beautiful and certainly rewarding.

My career has grown too. Since I finished college I went through some things trying to find my niche. I had been a secretary, most of the time an executive secretary, and I couldn't break out of the stereotype. I prayed and meditated and asked God to lead me where He wanted me to go. I've just received a nice promotion with my own office and I'm no longer a secretary. This has done wonders for my confidence, and most days I thoroughly enjoy my job. Sometimes the pressure gets rough and I ask God, "Where do You want me to be?" For now I feel He wants me where I am, and when He's ready to move me, I'll be ready. I'll do the leg work, and I'll let God handle the decisions.

I have grown much in the last seven years, much more than at any period in my life. I have experienced joy and serenity a lot in the last few years. I will continue going to meetings to maintain what I have received and to grow more. Also, if everyone had received help and quit going to meetings before I came to my first meeting, there wouldn't have been anyone there to help me and offer the gift of hope. Life keeps throwing new things at me, and I don't ever want to return to my old way of handling them. I still have some unsolved problems to work on, and some day when I'm ready I know God will remove them.

Today I love life and it's inconceivable that I once wanted to end my life. I am not afraid of death, because I have meditated on this and have received assurance from my Higher Power. I thank God for this beautiful Program and all the beautiful people who have become my friends in EA.

Barb

(12)

OVERCOMING OBSTACLES

I will start my story with a little about my childhood. I was a very shy little girl. It was pure pain for me to speak to someone I didn't know really well.

My father was an alcoholic but would not admit it or even try to quit. When he drank we had to hide the knives, guns, or anything else that was dangerous. He would become violent and beat my mother. Many nights my sisters and brother and I would be wakened by swearing and loud noises. We knew dad was drunk again. We also had to hide the liniment, vanilla, rubbing alcohol, and anything of that nature because when he was out of liquor he would drink anything. So a great share of my life was living in fear when my dad was drinking. We moved many times because my dad changed jobs continually. I believe I went to about nine different schools.

Due to my shyness I found this very hard. By the time I had made friends we would have to move again. Whenever we changed schools or Sunday Schools I would be sick to my stomach. One place we lived in was a huge house. Every evening I would be sick to my stomach and dizzy. Thank God we only lived there three weeks. The last time we moved was when I was thirteen. Then I went to the same school until I graduated. I was still very shy and didn't participate much in school activities.

When I was sixteen I started dating, which helped my self-image. I met my husband when I was eighteen and we were married three days before my nineteenth birthday. We lived on a farm and I fell in love with farming.

We had a beautiful baby girl during our first year of marriage. Our marriage was good although we had a lot of petty arguments. These probably were caused because I was immature and had a very bad temper. Having a baby in our first year of marriage also tied me down, and our financial situation was always strained.

Four years later we had another baby girl. A month after she was born I had my appendix removed. From that time on I started having problems with my stomach. The doctor said it was nerves and he started me on tranquilizers. These helped some.

I was really happy with just two children, but since we were on a farm my husband wanted a boy. Reluctantly I agreed. During my pregnancy I was having a nervous breakdown but didn't realize what was happening. I can't remember too much of that period because I was so medicated. I had tranquilizers of every sort, pills for nausea, and strong sleeping pills. I can remember I would get the two girls, who were then three and seven, ready for bed and write my husband a note telling him I was going to bed. During my pregnancy I spent most of the time in bed because I just could not function. I was very crabby and mean, although I knew I shouldn't be that way; but I couldn't stop it. When I was five months pregnant I was hospitalized for rest, but this didn't help. Finally our baby was born — a big, healthy baby boy. I know God was watching over him because even with all my medication, he was a normal baby.

I thought that once the baby was born I would be fine. Three weeks after he was born, my doctor and minister persuaded me to admit myself to a state mental hospital, but I did not realize where I was. They put me on medication and I saw my psychiatrist about two times while I was there. I went home after five weeks, but after thirteen days I started to vomit and couldn't stop. I returned to the hospital, thinking my medication would be changed. I was even willing to have shock treatments, but nothing was changed. When I couldn't keep the pills down I was given shots. My hips were so sore it hurt to walk. I would eat at meals and in between meals also, but the only thing that would stay down sometimes would be pop. One nurse insisted I eat in the main dining room. I would vomit in front of other patients and be so embarrassed.

I was there five months before I talked to a psychiatrist making the rounds in the day rooms. That was the only way you could get to talk to him because the hospital was so understaffed. He asked me how I was feeling. I told him and he looked at me very intently. He told the head nurse to change my medication to a new drug never before used on this particular ward. The very first pill I took that evening made me pass out, but I could feel my stomach starting to quiet down. After the third pill, I was able to eat a regular meal and have it stay down. A week after they changed my medication I was able to go home.

All the while I was in the hospital I was wondering why God was punishing me. I would ask my poor husband, "Am I really such a bad mother and wife that God is punishing me?" I would plead with him to take me home if he loved me. He couldn't because he saw no possible way I could function or get well. He was so loving and good to me, but he would be torn between trying to please me and doing what was best for me.

When I went home I still couldn't take care of my baby for another month. It seemed as if it took forever for some feeling of happiness to enter my life again. It was like a big empty vacuum. We had a hired girl so this allowed me to go in and out of the house as I pleased. When spring came I spent most of my time outdoors. I loved doing field work and nature had its way of healing.

About a year after I was home from the hospital we started square-dancing. This was my therapy at that time. We were out among people and formed some beautiful friendships.

In 1964 we had another baby boy. He was not planned for. He came along very unexpectedly, but he was a Godsend. I lived with the fear of getting pregnant and having another breakdown. My pregnancy had its bad moments but most of the time it was quite normal. For the first eighteen months our baby was sick. At three weeks he had a double hernia operation; then he had a very serious case of trench mouth, then chicken pox, and finally he had his tonsils and adenoids out. I took care of him and I never have regretted his being born. He was God's answer to my fear of getting pregnant and being able to take care of another baby.

In 1967 we sold our farm and moved to town. This was a drastic change for me. I thought all my neighbors would be close friends. Well, it just didn't turn out that way. So I retreated into the house and just went out when absolutely necessary.

I got the flu and became dehydrated, and this set off my depression again. Also, the pain from my hip and legs, which started after my last baby's birth, was very severe. With the combination of strong pain pills and other medication I began to hallucinate and have nightmares. Finally they took me to our town hospital in an ambulance. I was there three days when my doctor said I would have to go to a hospital where I could get help for my depression. This time it was not the state hospital because my husband's insurance would pay for most of the bill.

My psychiatrist put me on the same medication that made me vomit. I told him I was scared, but he said to see how it would work this time. After two weeks my stomach started getting queasy again and I couldn't sit down because I just had to keep moving. Finally they changed my medication but I was there five weeks. When I went home my depression started again. After three months I returned and this time was given shock treatments. When I went home I vowed I would never go back.

An AA member brought a member from a Twelve-Step Program for emotions to see me. She told me about the Program and asked if I would come. I agreed because I had been looking for something like this for years. My memory of just when I started isn't too clear, but I believe it was about 1970. My husband and I went together. I found a group of beautiful people — warm, friendly, and sincere. I also found I was not alone. At first I resented them because they were well and I was so sick, filled with self-pity and saying poor, poor me. In time that feeling left and I just felt love for them.

Through EA I have become closer to God. I always believed in God, but He was a punishing God and a God who just would not listen to my insignificant problems. Now I pray to God for everything and also remember to thank Him. My days seem to be a continual conversation with God. He is never very far from my thoughts. I ask Him to help me with my work around the house. If I'm going some place I invite God along — we go together. But if I start my day without God, something isn't right. I do not have the best day. So when I realize that I have forgotten God, I turn my will and life over to Him and ask Him for help.

Since I've been in EA my whole outlook on life has changed. I do not have to be the center of the Universe. Everything does not have to go my way all the time. I've turned my husband and children over to God. It is such a blessed relief to realize I can try and be the best wife and mother I can. If there are problems for them, it is not my responsibility to run their lives and to shield them from all their hurts and mistakes. God gives me my problems to grow so why should I begrudge the same for my family?

God has given me patience and understanding through EA and He gives me more insight into myself as time goes on. Without EA I'm sure I would probably have had another breakdown, but I have my God-given Program — Emotions Anonymous — and all my friends to help me when the rough times come. I thank God for EA, for all the progress I've made, and for all my wonderful EA friends.

Ardis

(13)

DON'T LET ANYONE SEE YOU CRY

Don't let anyone see you cry — what will people say?
Most of the days of my youth on the farm were spent hiding from someone or something. There were thirteen children
in our family and since I was the youngest of eight girls,
there was always a lot of activity.

When I was five, my sisters would have boyfriends come
over and since I was especially tiny, they constantly wanted
me to sit on their laps. Because they were drunk most of the
time, their actions really frightened me. The fear and negative thinking came upon me so quickly and I thought, "If
only someone would love me or defend me." With the beginning of third grade and already filled with fear and feelings of rejection, the horrible realization came that my dad
was an alcoholic. He never beat us physically but always
verbally with the exception of one time. He followed me into
the house with a horse whip and as he swung I jumped and
it hit mother right on her open sore on the leg. Dad turned
pale as mother was screaming, but he soon left the house and
didn't come back in for a long time. I didn't know how to
handle all the sick emotions that were coming to me. It
was difficult to understand why mother was crying so much
and trying so hard to please him.

I know now that I reacted, and not in a positive way.
"Why do I do some of these things like bedwetting until the
age of nine and why are there so many headaches and why
do I feel so sad and why is there never a word of praise or
thank you or any affection," I remember thinking. The
first time any affection was given was when mother held my

hand as she was dying of cancer when I was eighteen. These times I am sure that self-pity, resentments, guilt and fear came creeping in and I was not aware of any of them.

The experience I had with a teacher gave me a terrific struggle for about ten years when she said, "If you think something you do is a sin, it is a sin." I really let this sentence take complete control; everything became sinful and every time I didn't feel good I was so afraid to lie down, thinking I would die and that if I did die I would go to hell. I often wondered about sex but never let myself think or feel anything. I just hated my body; it was all so terrible and sinful. I remember praying that my body would never change because my older sisters were teased so much. When I was allowed to go to town I would drink huge amounts of alcohol and I soon noticed this gave me some relief from all those sick emotions but somehow I realized I would soon be like my father if I didn't stop.

Then I met this boy who now is my husband. I thought he seemed so strong, someone I could depend on, someone who would make me happy. This was also one sure way of getting away from the farm, and we were married, although I was not sure about my love for him. I'm sure I was so wrapped up in myself that I wasn't capable of a love that was needed for a good marriage. The first fifteen years I just existed, looking at surface things for happiness, but I was never sure or secure. I always thought a good wife would never talk back and I kept everything in and cringed when anger was expressed. I reacted to everyone's mood, but only inwardly. I worked so hard to put on a big front, even though I was hurting inside. A neighbor lady we had would sometimes build my self-esteem and the next day tear it down. I felt I had to be careful not to disappoint her, but finally I got so frustrated that I got away from the terrible hold she had on me.

Life then for a few years became bearable until one day there was a picnic at the lake. With us were two teenage boys who were over six feet tall and one of them was emotionally ill. At one time he had held a knife at his mother's throat for two hours as she felt she couldn't dare move from the couch. I had a horrible fear of water because of a local drowning experience in my teens, but this day slowly I went into the water and before I knew it, these two big guys came after me and held me under. The panic was horrible and I don't remember coming back to shore. Later that day a sick boy attacked our young son and left him on the shore black and blue — just shaking.

The next day early in the morning my husband had to call the doctor because of severe pain in my back from the tremendous struggle in the water so I was given pain pills and had to have treatments for a strained back. A few days after coming home, I suddenly had severe chest pains and couldn't breathe; panic again took over and I thought this was a heart attack. My husband took me to the hospital and I had to stay there three days, being released with tranquilizers. Everything looked so unreal I finally stopped taking them after a month. A few days later came a deep, severe depression, fear, anxiety, panic, with my whole body trembling, and I did not know what was happening or how to handle these strange emotions.

A different doctor was recommended by a friend. I was given more pills and by this time my weight loss was six pounds a day and I was so weak I barely made it into the office. The doctor took one look at me and said, "You're going into the hospital." I was given shots every two hours. Everything was a blur and I had this terrible sinking, sinking feeling. I thought maybe this was death. Two nurses came in and put me into an old-fashioned tub which was so deep that I fought because I thought they were going to drown me. I asked why I had to be put into the bathtub and they said, "Because you are going into an institution." I was so overwhelmed with fear because I thought the same thing was going to happen to me that happened in the movie, "Snake Pit." Coming to the state hospital was a nightmare. Seeing so many sick and retarded people with strange looks on their faces was all a new experience. Tension became so severe that muscle spasms took over until I couldn't walk and was put in a wheelchair for some time. I had to have someone dress me for six weeks. I couldn't sleep because of fear and migraine headaches, but somehow I did manage to go home in about seven weeks.

The next three years were really a struggle and the two after that I felt so good, I thought I would never be sick again. I started a course in beauty college but the strain and pressure and study in the evening while trying to keep house for four children and a husband were more than I could cope with. I even took more of my medication but nothing helped as all the same sick emotions again took a firm hold.

The doctor said I should again go into the state hospital for a change of medication. The withdrawal and trying new drugs was a painful experience and after a two-month stay, the adjustment was so difficult that I felt I'd have to be confined for a lifetime. I took a little more medication for the first week at home than was prescribed and gradually began feeling better.

The next few months a few positive thoughts were coming through that something better was going to happen and while looking in the paper, I noticed a big advertisement about an open meeting for EA. I called a few people I had met in the hospital to see if they would come along. I was a little leary as to what kind of people would be there, but when I met these people I felt as if I had known them forever and as I listened to the speaker, I knew they had something I wanted and needed.

It took a few years in EA before I could feel trust or acceptance or even receive the love these people were giving. It took still another year or so before I really believed in my heart that anyone cared.

I had spent many years being so proud of my Catholic background and was so sure all the other denominations didn't have a chance, but the Program gave me an open mind and now how I thank my Higher Power for this gift, this EA Program. I have been so blessed by people from each denomination and somehow I believed the words, "Ask and you shall receive, seek and you will find," but God seemed so far away.

I definitely didn't believe then that He cared about our little needs but His grace gave me the assurance there would be more and I didn't stop asking, "God, I want to be pleasing to you. What is your will for me? How can I get to know you or come close to you?"

I'm overwhelmed about the many things I have to be thankful for and how the Program gave me the desire to search. I have received something I never had before and that is confidence and self-esteem. I can't put into words the comfort I get from reading and praying with His word. "The truth shall set you free." No more need to feel rejected, no more starving for love, no more real loneliness, no more soul sickness or fear. I now have a good relationship with my husband and family and with God as the third party making it work these last six years.

Negative thoughts do come and will stay if I don't spot them and stop them by His power and the help of the great people in EA. I always try to start the day asking, dear Lord, let all be of You today, just today. I can now thank Him for emotional illness — it brought me from a lousy existence to a meaningful life. God has not called us to see through each other but to see each other through.

Eileen

(14)

I WAS ONLY CONNING MYSELF

I have been in EA for six years. I attend weekly meetings, I have a lot of telephone contacts with EA members, and I spend time reading Twelve-Step material and try to live the Program "one day at a time."

As a child I recall almost continual unhappiness and was constantly doing or saying things to get love and attention. Many times it meant lying in bed at night crying loud enough so my parents would hear me. I remember the disappointments, because they never seemed to hear and if they did, ignored it. The desire for attention at that time was so great, I remember actually praying for some sickness or disease. I had more infections from cuts by age eight than the average person has in a lifetime. And I mean they were cuts that I inflicted upon myself. That was severe emotional illness and that was also suffering.

I always felt there was something horribly wrong with me but I didn't know how to handle it. These are some thoughts that I continually lived with: What will we do tomorrow that will make me happy? Why are my brothers and sisters happy? What can I do to make my mom and dad like me? Why am I dumb in school? What is wrong with me? This was my unhappiness day after day.

When I graduated from high school I joined the convent at St. Benedict's College. I had a brother who was studying to be a priest and he got lots of attention and approval from home, so that was a sure thing for me, I thought. They saw through my unhappiness and after six months advised me to quit.

After this episode I spent about five years working in hospitals as a nurse's aide and did many things that are too gory to tell about and at this point in life are of no value to anyone to hear.

In 1962 I married a man who knew I had emotional problems but said he wasn't concerned about it. We were married four days and already I began playing sick games with him. I ended up in the hospital for a physical problem that I deliberately brought on myself. No one ever knew about it including my husband or the doctor.

From 1962 when we got married, to 1970 when I joined EA, I spent much time in Willmar State Hospital, Glenwood Hills Hospital, Abbott Hospital, Two West at St. Cloud, St. Mary's Hospital in Rochester and Anoka State Hospital. I had two major surgeries which would have never had to be. They were brought on by severe emotional problems. I had forty-eight shock treatments over this period of time. I was hooked on tranquilizers, anti-depressants, sleeping pills, and also began abusing pain pills such as demerol and codeine.

My husband had bought his own tractor-trailer for long distance moving and we had a good business. I could never accept his being gone and fought him all the way. He missed so much time from work because of my illness that we finally ended up in a bankruptcy, whereby we lost everything.

In January of 1970, a doctor advised me to go home and try to live with my illness as best I could and also to strongly consider getting a divorce. I did that. I came home, considered divorce, but more strongly than that considered suicide which I had tried but failed at twice already.

One day a friend, probably the only friend I had left at this point, stopped by the house and asked me to try going to EA meetings. She had seen it advertised in the paper and thought maybe it could help me. So I decided to try it just to please her.

For three months I went to weekly meetings and just listened. Sometimes I went home feeling worse than when I came in and sometimes I felt a little better. At many meetings I couldn't sit through them and just had to get up and leave. The next week I always managed to get back.

One EA member spent much time with me after meetings and on the telephone. I couldn't figure out why she liked me. If I worked hard at the Program she seemed to like that; if I played sick games with her she also seemed to accept that. I tested her friendship many times. After many tries at this type of thing I came to realize that if EA people care this much - then how much greater God must care. That EA member helped me to find my Higher Power.

The EA Program has taught me that I cannot change my husband, that I can only change myself. As a result, I have learned to accept the type of work he has, which in turn has brought us much closer together.

When I came into EA I had nothing. Today I have some peace of mind, and am striving for more, of course. We have a good marriage, three lovely children, and my husband and I are back in business.

I have found that the Program is not so much a way of learning new ideas for achieving happiness, but a means of getting rid of my past wrong ideas of how to achieve happiness. For instance, I used to think pills would make me a happier person, but I found that disciplining myself not to use pills makes me happier. I used to think if I could dictate to my husband as to how he should live and act I could be happier. Now I have found that if I let him alone and just concentrate on how I should live and act I am much happier.

One thing I like about this "live and let live" stuff is that it puts me out of the driver's seat. Before, if I ordered everyone else around and they didn't do what I wanted them to do, the result was an upset for myself. That is the area where I was creating my own problems.

The Program has also taught me to "look for the good." This last year has been a real struggle for me in the Program. My negative mind wants me to think that EA is a waste of time for me. But when I think of "look for the good," I can say I have had five good years in EA.

Even though I am having rough times I still will not

miss meetings. The group meetings give me the inspiration to continue to try to make this Program once again work for me. Before I was in the Program when things got rough, all I felt was despair; now I have lots to live for and that makes me happy.

The Twelve Steps to me are what a tool chest is to a carpenter. For every situation or problem I come in contact with in a day, there is always a tool to make things easier. For instance, I used to get hurt easily if someone said the wrong thing to me or about me. I would take it personally and probably fret over it for days. Now to get over such a situation I try to be aware that that individual is probably hurting pretty badly himself; then I do not have to take it as a personal thing.

I spent almost thirty years of my life doing things that harmed my physical and emotional self. Six years ago I first learned why I was doing these things. It was simply because I did not like myself. I took the Twelve-Step Program and the people to convince my that I am an okay person.

I would like to share with you one of the greatest moments in my life. The date was June 4th, 1972. I remember the date and time very well. That evening I was ready to take my Fifth Step. I called and made an appointment with a Fifth Step person and for some reason I felt strongly that my husband should be included in this. I felt it so strongly that I asked him to come along and he reluctantly agreed to. Up until this time I had done so many things that involved my husband which I felt had to go to the grave with me. I was always afraid to be honest with my husband. But now I had reached a point in my life where I felt secure in myself and knew I could tell him everything as well as suffer any consequences that might follow. From that point on our marriage was uphill all the way. As soon as I was honest with him, he also wanted to come closer to me. I have never verbally apologized to my husband for the times I wronged him. I have changed my ways. While taking my Fifth Step that night I actually felt the presence of God.

God will restore me to sanity but I must work the

Twelve Steps to the best of my ability and then I can "let go and let God." If I try to restore myself to sanity by my own desires I won't make it.

I still have times when I am struggling with the Program. But I am grateful for those times because I always learn something new. When I am with EA people I feel so much love. God is really alive and present in our Twelve-Step people and groups.

Kathryn

LIFE HAS JUST BEGUN

"You need to see a psychologist," said the chiropractor, after listening to my tale of woe. He went on talking, but I didn't hear him. My mind was in a whirlwind.

"He's put into words what I've been afraid to admit even to myself. I wanted so badly for it to be physical."

"A psychologist. Wow! So that's what's wrong with me. I'm crazy."

"This can't be happening to me. I'm stronger than that. What will I tell Bill when I get home? How can I tell him? What will happen to me? Oh, God, why did I come here?"

I came to this man for a magic answer but he wasn't giving me the right one. I wanted to run. But where to? I went home and didn't let on about anything. I was bursting at the seams the next day when I went to see my cousin, a nun who was visiting. I poured everything out to her — how I felt like crying all the time, how I didn't care if I ever got up in the morning, how I'd wish I hadn't awakened when I found myself awake, how I didn't want to see anyone or talk to anyone on the phone, how I felt as though I were in a cave and everyone else was walking past me, but I wasn't a part of where they were — and most of all, I talked to her about how scared I was to tell my husband. I was afraid he would be ashamed of me. After all, hadn't he shushed me up when my mom wrote saying my sister was in the hospital having shock treatments ten years before?

My cousin encouraged me to tell Bill right away and talked about some of the nuns she knew who had problems like mine. I listened but kept thinking, "Yes, but this is happening to me — right now." By the time I went home, I was convinced that I had to tell Bill. The next morning, Sunday, before going to church, I worked up the courage to ask Bill to come out into the kitchen to talk away from the kids. We sat down and I told him what the chiropractor had said. He looked at me with compassion and said, "If that's the kind of help you need, that's the kind of help you'll get." He held my hand while I cried. I felt so relieved. He hadn't turned against me as I was so sure he would.

In the next few days, I tried every avenue to prove the chiropractor wrong — I tried unsuccessfully to get an appointment with an eye doctor, because there seemed to be a shadow over my left eye — if I could only get rid of that, then I would be all right. Although I couldn't get an appointment with him I did talk to him over the phone. He said, "It sounds to me like you're having a nervous breakdown." That was not what I wanted to hear!

I fell apart and could hardly talk to our parish social worker when I called her. She came over immediately and I cried on her shoulder. She kept telling me that I would be okay.

But I wasn't okay — and time dragged on and on. The days were endless. I would sit in a chair by the kitchen table for hours, my mind racing but my body unable to move except to smoke cigarette after cigarette, and drink cup of coffee after cup of coffee. I finally gave in and made an appointment with our family doctor. I had to do something to get well. My kids needed me. The doctor told me I was depressed and recommended I see a psychiatrist. He tried to get me in that day, a Friday, but couldn't make an appointment until Monday. He gave me a prescription for what I thought would calm me down. I followed the directions wrong and wound up staying awake all night. I became so hyper that my eyelids would not stay shut, I even tried lying on my face. A thought I had was, "I can't tell anyone this or they'll know I'm crazy."

By the time I got to the doctor's office on Monday, I

was beside myself. What good would it do me just to talk to someone? The doctor asked me how I felt about being there. I said I was very scared, scared because he might put me in the hospital, the hospital that was visible through his office windows — the same hospital where my dad's four-year decline to death had begun.

After listening to me pour out some of my fears and things I had not told anyone before, the doctor said he didn't think I would need to be hospitalized. I could go home and start taking some pills he was prescribing. What a relief! I could call him whenever I felt I needed to talk to him.

In the next two weeks, I called four times and each time the medication dosage was changed. Those two weeks were pure "hell." I was depressed and anxious at the same time. I couldn't sit still and yet I was so down. I would have so much energy I would burn myself out. I dug the bulbs out of my garden with my bare hands because I had so much energy. Then I went in the house and collapsed. It was a hell of a way to get back on my feet, but it did the trick. I had some qualms about being a pill popper but I made a joke of it.

At first I saw the doctor every three weeks or so. I was able to tell him things I had never told anyone. To what seemed to me to be an impossible situation, he would say, "Either accept it or change it." I could see no way of doing either, so I continued to be frustrated.

I was told I had an anniversary syndrome, because I had gotten depressed in September, about the same time of year two years in a row. Around that time my dad had attempted suicide at my house by taking one hundred pills of different kinds. By summer I wasn't taking as many pills but when fall came around, I'd be back up to three pills a day. After three years of this, I was tired of having to rely on pills to get me through life. I wanted to live without pills. I began to voice this to my family and friends. "There must be some way for me to live without having to rely on pills." One day, a girlfriend of mine called and said she had something to tell me. She came over and told me about

Emotions Anonymous. I'd read an article in the local paper about it some time before. "That'd be a good thing for my sister to join," I'd thought at the time. Now my friend Gloria was telling me it might be for me. I thought it was a good idea and said, "Sure, let's go sometime."

We let it go until Gloria called one day. "They're having an open meeting next Saturday and we're going. But first let's go to a regular meeting." I was late and had to find the room by myself. I walked in while the meeting was in progress. Each person was taking a turn talking. When it came to my turn, I was told I could pass, or talk, or ask questions. I told of how involved I was in helping a member of my husband's family who was depressed. After the meeting, someone came up to me and asked, "Do you have to be that involved in someone else's life?" I had never thought I didn't have to be so involved. I didn't know I had a choice. I thought I didn't have that much to do with it. I now know I have a lot to do with the way my life is.

That was the first of many insights I gained in the first few months of going to weekly meetings. As I went, my mind began to clear and I could hear what the others were saying. I recognized myself in what they said. I belonged here because these people were saying out loud things I had hardly dared think to myself. They talked about feelings, emotions such as hatred, resentment, anger, self-pity, guilt, frustration.

I began to see that one of the reasons I had become ill was that I piled hurt upon hurt and would dredge up all the old hurts when a new one came along. The funny thing about resentment was that I thought I was hurting the person who had hurt me, and in reality I had only succeeded in harming myself.

Before coming to EA, the only emotion I could recognize in myself was anger. I knew I was powerless over that. When I was angry I had no control. I also thought I would go to a few meetings to find out how to change my husband and kids and then I would be happy. It didn't take long for me to realize that I couldn't change them — that I could only change myself. It was a disappointment and a relief at the same time.

And so it went through six months of regular attendance. Ups and downs. No easy answers but lots of insight coming fast and furious. I went from believing I was a "good" person to seeing myself as a "terrible" person who had lots of garbage to get rid of. I was encouraged to take a Fifth Step, which I did. The man I went to was very accepting and helped me put myself back into perspective. He helped me see I had done the best I could with what I had at the time. I felt so lifted after getting rid of all the garbage. I wasn't so bad after all.

And God loved me, period, not because I had done this or that or because I had not done this or that. He just plain loved me. I believe I began to love me, too.

I'd been in the Program a few months when our pastor announced one Sunday that a parishioner had been told on Christmas Eve that he had six months to live because of cancer. I wondered how that man must feel. I mulled that over and over in my mind. I tried to put myself in that man's place and became more and more obsessed with what having cancer would feel like. A few months later, I found out. Lymphosarcoma! "Does that mean cancer, doctor?"

"Yes, you have cancer, cancer of the lymph system, but it is one of the most treatable types to have. I know a woman who had this kind of cancer seventeen years ago and she is still alive and well."

"Help me, oh, God, help me," I cried as my knees buckled under me and I leaned heavily on my husband. Oh, did I feel alone and isolated. It was as though I were watching the scene from somewhere else. "This can't be real. Oh, God, I'll do anything for this not to be happening to me. Let me wake up from this nightmare."

But the nightmare was real. Thank God, I had someone to talk to about how I was feeling and about some of the screwy thoughts I was having. And to help me identify what I was feeling — fear, fear, and more fear — fear that made my skin crawl.

The few days I spent between surgeries (a biopsy and an exploratory operation) are a blur to me now. Besides taking a lot of pain pills at that time, I thought of myself constantly. One of those days was my husband's birthday. We had an impromptu party for him, but it's a blur to me now.

The exploratory surgery showed how bad it was. I was in the worst stage of the illness. After the surgeon talked to me, the chaplain came in. We prayed together, and then I was on the phone again with my EA friend, for the third time that day. I was reassured that it was okay for me to be afraid, for me to be angry, for me to cry, for me to be hopeful, to be despairing, to be whatever it was I was. The acceptance I got from her was something I'll never forget. We gained strength and faith in a Higher Power through each other. I began to experience the Spirit of this Program alive and living somehow in this relationship. I think I began to really live when I was afraid of dying the most.

"I'll be damned if I'm going to give up without a fight," I thought. Someone in the Program gave me an article to read about a woman with terminal cancer of the stomach who believed God could and would cure her, and she was cured. No trace. I read another article about someone who died of TB even though there was no medical reason for her death. I began to see how my attitude could help me or harm me.

Every six weeks, I would be in treatment for two weeks. Besides an injection each week, I took fifteen pills a day for the two weeks. At one point, I became addicted. When I stopped taking the pills at the end of the two weeks' treatment, I went from being very high to being very low within a few days. I wondered if I even were a human being. Fortunately, I was in touch with my EA friend. "Sounds like you're experiencing withdrawal symptoms. Get on the phone and call the doctor right now," she said. I called. After what seemed an eternity, the doctor called the next day. I was to go back on the pills and taper off by taking less and less each day. Within a week, I was feeling better and off the pills until the next treatment. Patience, reaching out to someone, and having the experience of facing withdrawal were some of the things I learned through that experience.

I believe the Program and the people in it are the reasons for my being alive today, over five years after that fateful day. The Program and the people have given me "tough love." Self-pity is destructive for me. I believe I could die from self-pity.

My friends in EA told me some things that were similar to shaking me by the shoulders till my teeth rattled: "Why do you think you're so unique? We're all dying a little each day." "It isn't how long we live. It's how well we live." "You probably have every right to feel sorry for yourself, but what good is it doing you?"

I learned to live one day at a time, to cherish each hour, to share my thoughts and feelings when I can with others, at meetings, on the phone, when visiting my EA friends, and with my family. I've found that those closest to me are the hardest for me to be close to.

I believe I had cancer of the soul long before I had cancer of the body. Resentment, anger, and self-pity ate at my spiritual fiber. Before EA I was as unaware of the destruction these emotions caused as I was of the cancer before it was brought to my attention.

Through the help of the Twelve-Step Program of Emotions Anonymous, I have not gotten rid of my feelings for then I surely would be dead, but I have found a way to deal with them. I've learned to pay attention to what's going on inside of me, to share my inside with others, to accept my feelings as just that — feelings. They are a part of who I am.

I've learned to live not just to exist. I've found a reason to live and life is full, one day at a time. Today — this is all I really have — I am alive and I want to live while I am alive. The treatments worked wonders. Today there is no trace of cancer. I am tremendously grateful for being alive, but I am even more grateful for being happy while living.

To me the miracle is not only that I am alive, but that I can be and am happy most of the time. I'm not only living, I am alive — alive with feelings, emotions, and an inner spirit that I'm learning to share.

I believe love has a part in healing, whether it's physical healing or emotional healing. I believe the acceptance and love I've received in EA through the people my Higher Power has sent into my life, and the potent drugs used to kill the cancer, have saved my life. Through the help of EA, I'm learning to love, not only others but myself as well, probably the hardest one of all for me to love.

My story doesn't have an ending. It's a never-ending process of learning and living — of falling down and getting up again. The Program has turned me on to life and I'm deeply grateful.

Helen

(16)

NO LONGER ALONE

I would like to begin my story about forty years ago. I know now that I was an emotionally disturbed child, teen-ager, and adult. Before I belonged to EA, I thought it was everyone else's fault and that I had good cause to act the way I did. I was a selfish, resentful, and withdrawn child. I was always jealous of my two sisters. I was very nasty to them and tried to blame everything I could onto them. I felt my parents loved them more than they did me. Natur-ally, I resented my parents too. Friends and relatives often remarked that I was the different child in the family. Being super-sensitive, I was crushed by those remarks and felt they didn't like me either.

When I was thirteen years old my brother was born. My parents were very busy people and being the oldest child in the family, I took care of my new brother a lot. I loved him like my own child and was very pleased that he liked me more than my sisters. He was my world until I was about fifteen years old. At fifteen my parents couldn't do much with me. I did all sorts of crazy things. I would tell terrible lies and skip school. Playing sick was one of my favorites because I would get a lot of attention. I also discovered alcohol, boys, and wild parties. I thought I finally found what I was looking for and what made me feel good.

At the age of sixteen, I became pregnant and was mar-ried. Neither my husband-to-be nor I wanted to get married, but we thought it was the only way out. I was a child go-ing to have a child. I was very sick during most of that pregnancy; consequently, I didn't care about anything at that point in my life. In a few months, I had a son who was born with many physical defects and was hospitalized several times. At the age of seven months, being a very weak child, he contracted pneumonia and died. I felt very guilty. I felt I didn't care for the child properly and that I was being punished for the awful things I did in my life. At this time, I was four months pregnant. It seemed like an eternity waiting for the child to be born. Would it be normal? Would it be a boy to replace the one I had lost?

After months of impatient waiting, God gave me a lovely daughter. I was disappointed it wasn't a boy and I still felt guilty, but was happy that it was a healthy child. I was a nervous wreck taking care of my new daughter. I had a hard time accepting the responsibility. It was so easy to take her to her grandparents' house. I knew they took good care of her. This also left me more time to spend with my husband, and I did a lot of drinking with him. I thought this would help our already unstable marriage.

This went on for four years and I became pregnant again. I just knew this child was going to be a boy — my second daughter was born. Again, I was very disappointed. I actually blamed my husband because it was a girl. Now, I had the responsibility of two children. I felt very tied down. I couldn't leave two children with the grandparents, so this meant I had to stay home and care for them. Meanwhile, my husband went out drinking and having a good time by himself. There were many problems, arguments, and my husband was staying away from home as much as possible.

This went on for four more years and I became pregnant again. I just knew this child would be a boy and would help improve our marriage — my third daughter was born. Everyone knew how disappointed I was. To make matters worse, my two sisters whom I was so jealous of each had two boys. My marriage was getting progressively worse as was my mental illness. I became pregnant again. This time, I did not care if it would be a boy or girl. My marriage was so bad and I was so physically ill (which was caused by my emotions) that I felt I could not handle another child. I did everything in my power but jump off the roof to prevent that child from being born. In spite of all my efforts, I had a healthy son.

Now, I thought all my problems would be solved. I had the boy and I was sure my marriage would improve, but things got progressively worse. I started taking pills to help me feel better. Then my brother, who was just twenty-one years old and was as close to me as my own children, was killed in an auto accident. This is when I started to hit the pills regularly and heavily. Sometimes, I would spend days on the davenport, while the children cared for themselves. My husband was spending more and more time away from home. Finally, he walked out on me. He found someone else and decided to marry her. This is when I hit my bottom. I didn't know which way to turn. I could not function. I had lapses of memory. I went through the entire Christmas season and had no recollection of any part of it. People would tell me they would be talking to me and all of a sudden I would just get up and leave. I do remember that I wanted to die. I guess I would have tried to end it all, but was afraid I would fail at that, too. I tried one desperate measure after another, going to one person after another, thinking surely one of them would have the answer for me. My second daughter was hospitalized due to a nervous condition. The children were terrified. One parent was gone and one was unstable. They had no idea what would happen to them.

I knew I had to do something. I contacted a friend and asked her questions about this EA she belonged to. She took me to my first EA meeting on New Year's night, four years ago. I didn't know it then, but it was a glorious way to start the new year. Before arriving at the EA meeting, I had pictured a bunch of people with eyes bulging out of their heads. Instead, I found a group of friendly, smiling faces. They made me feel warm and accepted. They made me feel that it was okay to be me. I knew this was what I wanted.

I kept coming to the meetings and started to work the Program, one day at a time. Every meeting I went to I learned more. I learned that God works through people. Time after time someone had just the right thing that I needed to hear.

I need to come every week to the EA meeting to "recharge" my battery. This is the place I found my Higher Power. He was always there waiting to help me, but I would not let Him. I thought I could handle my life. I always knew my Higher Power existed, but thought He was way up there and I was down here and I would handle things here. I not only tried to run my own life; I tried to run a lot of other people's lives, too. I am very grateful to my Higher Power that He did not give me all the ridiculous things I asked for. If I had gotten them, I couldn't have handled them. God knows what is good for me; I don't.

As I put myself in God's hands, a miraculous transformation took place in my life. My resentments, self-pity, jealousy, hatred and abnormal fears were disappearing. I saw things I had never seen before. A lot of the negative parts of my life were disappearing. I was having peace of mind. What a relief! What a burden lifted! As I improved, my children became much closer to me. They seemed to actually enjoy being around me. At an earlier time, they would stay as far away from me as possible. I now have a good relationship with my sisters and parents. When I was in my self-made hell, my sisters and parents were very kind and were the first ones to come to my aid.

So many good things have happened in my life after I got out of the driver's seat and let God do the driving. I went back to school and found a good job right in my home town. I met a man who didn't know anything about EA, but lived EA all his life. We were married in September of last year. My children and I love him very much.

I express my gratitude every day to God for all the blessings He has bestowed upon me. I express my gratitude for lifting the fog. I am thankful for all the beautiful things I now enjoy, like beautiful flowers, buildings, two lovely, lovely grandchildren, and many more things.

My Higher Power is my daily guide. Sometimes I get back in the driver's seat again. As a result, my character defects slowly creep back and I am miserable again. Then, I know it is time to get back to God and let Him take over. I still have many unsolved problems, but, through the EA Program, I am able to live at peace in spite of them. I have to thank God for all the obstacles He has put in my life as these were opportunities for me to grow, to make me better, not bitter. Through the Program I have found the greatest friend of all — my Higher Power. I have found a loving God, not a punishing God. I have many conversations with Him, not just the routine prayers I used to offer. I know He is here with me in everything I do. I shall never be alone anymore. He loves even me . . . .

Marlys

(17)
I BLAMED EVERYBODY ELSE

I'm Margaret S. and I have emotional problems.

Before EA my life was a miserable existence. I have been in Emotions Anonymous two years and I feel I'm two years old. Life is worth living the biggest percentage of the time.

I come from a middle class home. I had all the advantages as I grew up, but ever since I was small I can remember being upset and in turmoil inside. Before EA I blamed my unhappiness on old teachers, my parents, anyone, but never myself. My attitude was "Poor me, look at what the world is doing to me." Before EA I was paralyzed by a number of things. I was depressed most of the time. I had a lump in my throat that felt as if I could cry at any time. I went to many different doctors, but when they couldn't find any reason for all my aches and pains, they would offer tranquilizers. I would then become upset with their suggestions, quit going to them, and find a new doctor. My days were spent in front of the television. I didn't keep house or do much of anything. I was quite the party girl; I drank too much and couldn't keep that under control. To the outside people I was a happy-go-lucky person, but at home I was a screaming nut. I was always late for everything. I gossiped a lot about everyone. I belittled my husband all the time. I had one close friend and I let her abuse me and my family for years. Actually I thought I was a pretty good person. I couldn't figure out why my husband didn't think I was. I was also filled with a lot of different fears, such as a fear of the dark. I tend now to forget all of these things.

Enough of looking back. Like a girl in our EA group says, "It's not good to look back a lot." Anyway, I met a girl in my neighborhood who belonged to EA and she invited me along. My first impressions were good. However, I really felt my husband could use this Program more than I. EA taught me I had a choice. It showed me there is a God who loves me. It taught me how to hand my defects over to God. It showed me that honesty is the first rule to happiness. The "Just For Today's" were what caught my eye first. They really helped right away. The group I belonged to read out of the AA *TWELVE STEPS AND TWELVE TRADITIONS* book. Each week as we read the Steps in detail it felt as though that book was written about me. Slowly a curtain seemed to open. I saw who I was, what I was, and saw the choices I had. How beautiful to feel in control most of the time, as long as I handed the controls to God. I have gone down since I've been in the Program, but the period of depression wasn't as bad as before, and this time I had EA friends to help me through it.

I found God because I saw Him in the conscience of my group. I slowly started to tell them my fears and the things I hated about myself. They would tell me they, too, had these feelings. They still cared about me even after hearing these terrible things about me. Well, I figured if they loved me even after hearing these things, then the God they spoke about could too. Like they would say, "God doesn't make junk."

As I slowly began to love myself, I also began to see more good in others. My life changed greatly. I would say seventy-five percent of the time my defects are in God's hands. I know I'm far from finished working on myself. Through this Program I am much happier than I ever thought possible. My marriage is good; with God everything is better.

Spiritual awakening to me means a change in my personality. I have changed. My priorities are finally in place. I do have a spirit that needs to be taken care of each day in order for me to be healthy and happy. I thank God for EA and the beautiful people in this Program. I never realized when I started in this Program how much a new way of life meant. Now I know if I stay with the EA Program, which means close to God, with the support of my EA friends, I will have this new way of life.

In turn, I hope I can help other sufferers to realize there is another way to live this life. I hope I can spread the message to them; my own life will be the biggest example. With God all things are possible.

Margaret

(18)

THE KING RESIGNS

My story is based upon what I used to say others had done to make my life miserable. I started to run away from being married. I was emotionally, mentally, and spiritually divorcing myself from my wife because she had an emotional breakdown. Her illness was affecting me and the family. I would come home from work, go directly down to the amusement room and fill myself up with "false courage" and if it didn't take effect, I would add to it some hay fever pills to quiet me down.

I was developing psychosomatic symptoms, such as low back pain, burning and twitching eyes, impaired hearing, sensitivity to loud noises which produced headaches, sweating, and fever.

Sometimes I could not even walk to the supper table after trying to fortify myself against my wife. One night after I had gone through my routine of disassociation, I was dozing in the easy chair in the living room when she called that dinner was ready. I tried to get up only to land on my knees. I crawled on all fours to the kitchen, unable to rise because I had taken an over-abundant combination of whiskey and pills.

I didn't realize it then but I dominated my household, filled it with fear because of my awful temper. I was great at practicing character assassination and had to tear down others in order to build myself up. My ego could not be questioned. I was self-centered, interested only in my own gratification, and if I didn't have my way, I would throw a fit. I would walk out of the house and give my wife the cold, silent treatment. No one could cross me. No one could run the household like me. I didn't trust my wife's judgment in anything, ignored all her personal achievements, and made her my servant.

I made all the decisions and most of them were wrong. I felt the world was wrong and people were out of step with me. In truth, it was the other way around. I was out of step with the world.

I was argumentative and would always try to have the last word. I needed to win all the time. Everything was a life or death matter and I fumed when I did not get my way. I never shut off my emotional motor and was always on stage, putting on an act. I was loud, boisterous, and everyone knew when I was around.

My moods ran from high hilarity to my lower lip drooping down to the kitchen floor. I was critical and jealous of others because I did not feel equal to them. I was always mentally comparing and wishing for things I did not have. My work reflected my attitudes; it was erratic.

I always had a nervous stomach. I used big words to impress people and enjoyed pushing people around and seeing them cringe. I could not afford the risk of being hurt or of letting people find out I was just putting on an act. I didn't want people to know me because they might hate me and I had to have people around me proclaiming what a witty and clever fellow I was.

How hard I worked at being obnoxious just for the attention it brought me! I craved this attention and went to any means and lengths to achieve it. Mine was a hunger for recognition.

Nights were my enemy. I had to seek out people to keep the hectic pace alive. I had to go, go, go. There was no rest until I was worn out and could fall asleep from sheer exhaustion. I was running myself to death, running away from me. Anxiety was a normal state. I was always on edge waiting for something to happen. I used to wish for something to occur either good or bad so I would not have to stand still and wait.

I drove my car as if I were a tiger behind the wheel cursing at other drivers.

One night when I was reading the paper I glanced through the personal column. One ad appealed to me. It read, "Do you have a problem? Call number xxxx." I called this number and the person at the other end of the line told me it was Alcoholics Anonymous and they met on Friday nights.

I said, "Whoa, wait a minute. I am not a boozer. I am just having family problems."

"Oh, that's okay," she replied. "Lots of people use AA to straighten out their lives, even if they don't drink. You're welcome." I shall always be grateful to dear Annie.

I started attending meetings each Friday and also attended other AA groups. Gradually I came to grips with myself and my life started to straighten out. Although my home life was still a mess, I had gained a measure of serenity within myself.

One night I read another article in the paper about a group which meets for people who have emotional problems. Naturally I had to go. I was still looking for the answer. I didn't know yet that the answer was within me. I only had to look inside. I listened to those people at the meetings talk about how they had been before the Program and how they were now. Somehow, this sounded like the same thing I heard in the AA meetings, but I was impressed. Maybe there was some truth to it. Maybe if I kept an open mind something of value just might drop in.

My recovery was an inch-by-inch growth with blocks thrown all over my route. I recall the very first time I tried to tell the group about my past. I nearly choked on the words. I couldn't believe it was me talking. I didn't bare myself completely as I had not yet reached the point where I could trust people with my innermost feelings. Gradually I felt at ease with the group and with myself "telling it the way it was before EA and how it is now."

I tried changing myself in little ways first, such as "car driving." Then I let people get ahead of me in line. I opened doors for my wife. I tried not to practice character assissination when I was thwarted in business or at home. I used vocal restraint in disagreement. I practiced these actions until they became second nature, and lo and behold my life was becoming more manageable. These were some of the beginning things that led to a more serene and peaceful existence.

I had always wanted to be one of those persons who appears to have complete command of himself. My emotional make-up is not like that, but I have learned to start accepting myself for what God made me and live within that framework. I have learned to practice being more thoughtful of others by not deliberately going out of my way to harm them. This does not mean that I am a "human doormat" who has to buy love.

I learned two things very quickly when I came into the EA Program; first, "I must learn to listen, then listen to learn." I found out that if I don't get my way the world will not fall apart; the world does not revolve around me.

If some people during the course of the day are not so pleasant, I don't react with anger. I try pacing my work; but I try to work "First things first;" this does not mean I never procrastinate, however.

My life is no longer a roller coaster; my moods are more stable; I live on a more even keel.

My psychosomatic illnesses are a thing of the past. I have more energy to work and play. I am no longer filled with internal conflict and my frustrations are down to a minimum.

My attitude toward my children is more understanding and is not one of the "Lord and Master." I try to be a human being to my children; I treat them with respect and in turn I receive respect.

I have tried to let go and let God do His work. By letting go, I mean I don't have to control. I can let the natural order of events take place. I have stopped forcing. If I were to describe the transition that has taken place, I would say it went from a blackboard black to a sky blue or from harshness to softness. Even my marriage has become a "honeymoon."

So in the meantime, I attend EA meetings for insurance for my serenity. I owe my life and my marriage to EA, for without it I would have perished. I have been transformed into a resonably nice person and I like myself that way.

John

(19)

PEOPLE PLEASER

I grew up in a small Minnesota town, had a happy, secure childhood with normal ups and downs. I moved to the cities in December of 1962. I met my husband and married in 1964, bought a house in the spring of 1966, had a baby girl in the fall of 1966. In January of 1968 I had a son. All these are the makings of a very, normal, happy couple. But I was never completely happy within; I never knew why and just figured that was life. I never shared with anyone how I felt because I figured no one would understand because I didn't understand. I kept it all within me.

I couldn't see any reason to be unhappy, but I was. I couldn't share my feelings with my husband; he would get mad and yell at me, so I retreated more within. He couldn't seem to accept me as me, so as a result neither could I. I kept trying to please him and I never could. I would never make a decision for fear it would be wrong and then I would get yelled at again. What a circus!

Then I met someone else who liked and accepted me as I was so I asked my husband for a divorce. My husband thought we had a good marriage because I kept my mouth shut never telling him how I felt inside. I was too scared to tell him.

After I asked for a divorce, we started fighting. I started drinking more for the courage to tell him how I felt. After each fight I was emotionally drained and would be very tired. For all the peace we had in the first years of our marriage, our fighting made up for it from April of 1972 to August of 1972. In August we decided to separate; neither one of us could take the fighting anymore. It was very painful.

That same day in August of 1972 a friend of mine called and wanted to know if I wanted to go to an EA meeting, so I went. Since April she had asked me to go with her, but I had told her I had marital problems, not emotional ones. I never connected the two.

I can still remember the friendly people at my first EA meeting. Love came from these complete strangers who seemed to accept me as I was; that didn't seem possible when people who knew me didn't love me. So I kept going to meetings at first, for the love and acceptance, and I took my share. I liked being with people who told how they felt inside and not just said meaningless words. I came to realize "I was not alone" like I had thought I was. They all seemed to accept me more than my own family. I felt like I had come home. They all seemed so honest.

One night I sat in front of the slogan "Know Thyself-Be Honest." I didn't even know what it meant, but I worked on that slogan and came to realize it meant me and how I felt. Then I realized I had been a people-pleaser since my childhood. I never developed emotionally because of it. I would be what anyone wanted me to be. I had no idea who I was. I began to stop and think about what I was doing, and when I did something, I would try to understand why I was doing it. I found that I was completely controlled by other people, their actions and moods. If they felt bad I felt bad. I had always thought that to be good, one had to put others first. But it says, "Love your neighbor as yourself" — you can never love anyone if you do not love yourself first and if you are not in control of your own life.

So I kept going to weekly meetings. I thought I was a Christian before EA. I went to church every Sunday and did everything I was supposed to do, like pray. But soon I came to realize that the God in EA was not the same God as I had thought of Him before. I found a God in EA who cared every day about all the little things in my life. I learned to meditate and have a conscious contact with God and learned to turn my life and will over to Him twenty-four hours at a time. I learned to live one day at a time which I had never done before; I always lived in the past or the future, but never today.

I have to ask each morning for the next twenty-four hours, and thank Him each evening for whatever passed that day. Each day is a new life; one can never live on yesterday's success. I also came to realize I was spiritually dead before EA.

My husband and I decided to try it again after having been separated six weeks. Deep within, I did not give it much hope, but with living one day at a time, the Serenity Prayer and the first and second Just For Todays, I got through weeks, months and finally a year, which I feel took a miracle, considering how I felt before EA. Now it's been four and a half years and I feel they've been the best, at least the most honest ones.

In August of 1973, I attended my first EA Retreat and the theme was, "Let God Be God," a saying I have come to hold very dear to my heart. It became another turning point in my life and marriage. I only realized then that God allows us all our problems for a reason, to wake us up however·He can. So we have to permit each person to carry his own burdens. I will help anyone whenever or wherever I can, but I don't try to solve his problems for him. I let God be God; I only want to be His instrument. If He wants to use me in some way, I am available.

For I can see and thank God for every problem I've had, because without them, I would never have the peace and serenity I have today and I would not have EA and the beautiful people who make EA what it is. I know God led me into EA before I had an emotional breakdown. I was in the hospital once in April of 1972 for stomach pains, which were diagnosed as nerves after I told the doctor I was having some marital problems. I took half of the Valium, and the pain left and never has returned. I never took any more pills, so I feel God has spared me more hospitalization.

I live in a very real world now, no more daydreams or fantasies. I try to accept people as they are and only try to change myself by taking my inventory.

Since EA four and a half years ago, I've quit smoking and drinking. I realize I used drinking either for escape or for courage, and that can just lead to more problems. I have to face and accept my emotions honestly and head on. I can't run away from them; they are part of me. I've learned to like myself for, "God doesn't make any junk." I've learned to accept where I'm at in the Program today. Sometimes I fall but I always pick myself up and go forward. It's not been easy, but it's been worth every moment. I've stopped looking for happiness; I've found it. I've found EA; I've found God and I've found life. A personal God is who I was looking for all along.

To continue to grow, I go to weekly meetings, do volunteer work at the International Office, attend retreats, am on telephone-answering service, share whenever I can. Freely I have received, freely I give, and I always get so much more than I give.

If I've helped one person by sharing my story, then it's been worth it all. I hope to continue to grow in EA until I leave this world.

Fay

(20)

MY SELF-MADE WALL

My story is not a dramatic one. It does not have any overwhelming highs or dramatic lows. It is simply an example of the everyday pain and suffering that can come from being "powerless over our emotions."

I learned at a very early age to depend on the approval of others for satisfaction and to set unreasonably high standards for myself that I could not live up to. When I was born, in addition to my parents there were seven other adults in the house — a set of grandparents, three uncles, and two aunts. Although I have only very vague memories of my pre-school years, I am certain that I experienced many rewards for being a good girl. Conversely, I also feel I must have learned quickly what were bad things to do.

Looking back, I cannot remember very many happy days during my school years. At the time I was too proud to admit, even to myself, the discouragements and humiliations that I felt. From the time I started school, it was obvious that I was a better student than my classmates, and at the end of second grade I was double promoted. From that time on I felt like an outcast. Somewhere around the time I was ten or eleven, I decided that the reason I didn't have any friends was that I was ugly. I could not imagine that there was anything I was doing that would turn people against me, for I was always concerned with what was the right and proper thing to do. I quickly developed a facade of "I don't care, I don't need you," and went on to attempt to impress everyone with my intellectual abilities and my musical talents. Needless to say, no one was impressed and

181

by the time I reached high school, things had gotten a great deal worse. In the wisdom of adolescence, I now excused my unpopularity with not only my ugliness, but also the jealousy my schoolmates felt for my abilities. Even though I consciously depended on these excuses, I know I was haunted by some kind of deep-seated feeling that I was not okay, that I was an odd ball and would never be happy like other people. So the mask went on and stayed on. I had to pretend that I was happy with things as they were. In my state of self-centeredness, I felt many times that people were making fun of me, and my defenses became greater. I am certain that many other teenagers have gone through some of the experiences that I went through, but at the time I was convinced that I was unique — everyone else had it much better.

All of this, with occasional brief respite, carried over into my adult life. My college days started off in the same fashion. However, late in my freshman year I secured a part-time job where I was able to establish friendship with some of the people I worked with. I was still unable to reach out for a close friendship, but at least on a surface level, my rapport with others my age had improved. I learned what it was like to enjoy a party. I found I was able to sit down and carry on a conversation with others without having to impress them with how smart I was. In spite of the improvement in these relationships, I still carried the underlying feeling that they really didn't like me; they were just tolerating me. But things were better and I began to concentrate more on enjoying myself and less on my education. This led to guilt in future years because, although my work was certainly adequate in college, I had not distinguished myself academically.

Because of my fear of failure, when I planned my college program, I stayed away from the areas I was most interested in — mathematics and music — and decided to become an elementary teacher. I spent eleven years teaching school. During these years all of my insecurities surfaced at various times, some more than others. I began to realize how much

I wanted to experience close friendship and love, but did not know how to go about accomplishing this and did not really believe it could ever happen. Even when I would find people receptive to me, I would sooner or later exhibit some of my old character traits that were not appealing to others — gossip, criticism, superior attitudes. It is only after my experiences in EA that I am able to recognize these behaviors as contributing to my need to build myself up by tearing others down. This kind of behavior was upsetting to me. I had set standards for myself that included doing and being everything that is good and noble, and I often would spend an evening going over my deeds and words for the day and pick out what I had not liked. But this did not change my actions the following day; it just led to more dissatisfaction with who I was. When I could not live up to the impossible standards I had created, my self-hate grew.

During all these years, I had no idea that I had any emotional problems. I could go on and on listing all the things that today so apparently point to these problems, but I am writing my story, not a book. I had no symptoms that would indicate to me or anyone else that I needed help. I went to work every day, served on various committees, directed a children's choir, attended social functions, and was probably regarded as very independent and fairly successful. After growing up in a very poor home and scrimping and saving to put myself through college, I had acquired a measure of financial independence.

One of the biggest voids in my life was, I felt, that I wasn't dating anyone regularly or married like most of the women I knew. I had not dated at all in high school and only occasionally in the following years. As much as I would have liked things to be different, I knew it was hopeless. If someone did show an interest in me, I began to wonder if he was just as big a "loser" as I was, or what his motives were. Because I accepted, as have so many other women, the age-old theory that a woman without a husband and family is nothing, I felt I was a failure.

In spite of all my defenses, I met someone who was

willing to probe beneath my superficial aloofness and find the warmth and love that had been buried for so long. Eight months later we were married and as in the fairy tales should have lived happily ever after. I had what I thought I wanted more than life itself, love and the security of having someone to care for me. Life was beautiful for awhile. My career was no longer important to me. I began to be very dependent on my husband. If he was late getting home from work, I fretted. If he wasn't quite as affectionate as he had been, I cried. If he didn't compliment the way I did something, I felt I was no good. When I was out alone I started to experience strange physical sensations. I was attending graduate school and noticed some discomfort in walking to class. Some days I wasn't sure I would make it. Driving home one day, I experienced what I know now was a severe anxiety attack and thought I was going to die. I managed to get home where I called my husband and my doctor. My husband came home from work and went to the drugstore to pick up my doctor's answer, a prescription for Valium. For three and a half years I was to depend on this pill to try to get me through the tough moments, which occurred more and more often.

When school started in the fall, things weren't the same. I found I was constantly plagued by an ache in the back of my neck. I also experienced extreme panic and shakiness. I found it much harder to cope with the students and was not really satisfied with my performance on the job. Several times I went to my doctor, but he could find nothing wrong. I had decided earlier that this was going to be my last year of teaching and looked forward to staying home, expecting that would take care of my problems. It didn't, and I found, if anything, the symptoms got worse. After six months, I decided to go back to work on a part-time basis. Things got a little better for awhile. During that time my father died and I found, to my surprise, that I was able to handle the situation very well. I then took a full-time job which I found very tedious, unrewarding, and offering no challenge. I also found that once again the symptoms got worse. Several times when I had to take a bus to work, I again encountered all the anxiety symptoms and feared that I would not reach my destination.

By this time I had changed doctors, and this time the doctor suspected that the cause was not physical. Finally, after a series of tests and waiting to see if thyroid medication would have any effect, he decided I should be admitted to the psychiatric section of a hospital. I was more than willing to go. I still felt there must be a physical cause for my suffering, but knew that by hospitalization I would go through x-rays, and so forth, and they would find out what was really wrong with me. To my surprise, there was not a tumor or any other physical cause. I had to face the fact that my problems had an emotional basis.

I do not look back on my sixteen days in the hospital as having put me on the road to feeling better, but I was able to unload some of my guilt from the past, and I also began to overcome my dependence on Valium. The most positive thing that happened to me in the hospital was that twice my doctor had me attend orientation meetings where members of Emotions Anonymous came to the hospital and told how they had found help through the Program.

When I was released from the hospital feeling no better than when I went in, I decided I had nothing to lose by going to an EA meeting, which I did the first Saturday after I came home. I found hope. I went back and after several weeks of encouragement by the other members, I found the courage to go back to work.

During those first weeks or months of attendance at meetings, I was not really able to get in touch with any of the Steps of the Program other than Step One. But during that time I did receive many benefits. I learned that other people had the same suffering I did and had survived. Through the insight others had in themselves, I was able for the first time in my life to recognize some of my character defects and feelings which had caused me so much unhappiness and suffering in the past. I began to realize that what I had thought to be my unhappy lot in life through my early years, was only a result of my innermost feelings and could have changed if I had had the insight and hope the Twelve-Step Program brings.

Any insight I might now have into my behavior during all the years previous to EA is only a result of what I have learned in EA. As I continued to attend meetings, I became aware of more and more things that affected my ability to live a happy life. I learned that there was no virtue in all the worrying I had done. It did not prove to my husband or family how much I loved them. I learned that my constant striving to be the best played a big role in my illness. I learned about resentment, pride, fear, and many other character defects that had only been words to me before. I certainly had not been able to see them in myself.

As I became more involved in the Program and started to try to work the Steps, I had a great deal of difficulty with the spiritual side of the Program. Even though I had attended church regularly as a child and adolescent and played the organ for services, it had all been a ritual and part of doing what was expected of me. I had no real concept of God, and envied the people in the Program who were so comfortable in their relationship with a Higher Power. Through the Program, I have slowly learned that there must be a power greater than I, and although I still have not been able to clearly identify my Higher Power, I know it is there.

As I write this, I am nearing my fourth anniversary in the Program and I can see how my life has changed. The major change has been in my relationships with other people. I no longer refuse to reach out to someone because of fear of rejection. I also no longer constantly feel that I have to prove something to everyone. I am not afraid to let people know what I really feel.

I have made a good start on a second career. After leaving teaching, I floundered around for several years looking for the right job. Today I have a position that has been created in part by me as a result of the confidence I have gained in myself through the Program.

My marriage has grown through these years. Even during the most severe times of my illness, I was able to count on my husband for support. As I have learned to be an independent person and at the same time allowed my husband the same right to his individuality, our relationship has grown stronger.

My relationship with my mother and brothers has improved a great deal because I no longer become defensive at anything they might say that could be interpreted as criticism. I no longer live in fear of making a mistake, for I am beginning to accept that I am human.

In spite of all the growth that has occurred and self-knowledge I have gained, I still am and will continue to be powerless over my emotions. The longer I am in the Program the more I recognize my need to continue in it. It is too easy for me to backslide into my old habits of thinking and behavior. I need the weekly meetings to remind me of where I have been and where I could go back to if I don't remain diligent in my attempts to practice the Program.

EA is not just a Program where I go once a week to meet with other people. It has become a way of life for which I shall be forever grateful.

Jan

(21)

I COULDN'T ESCAPE FROM ME

Mine is a sordid story. I'm not proud of it, but I'm no longer ashamed of it. There's nothing pretty or exotic about it, but if it will help one person to avoid the mistakes I have made or to learn from the growth that I have made, then it is worth telling.

I believe it was about nine years ago that I began to get hints that all was not right with me emotionally. At least I became aware of the hints. I am sure there had been signs prior to that, but I ignored them.

At about that time, my husband and I began to move with a different circle of friends. Anyway, we called them "friends." They were oddballs and I guess we were attracted to them because they were so different from any other people we had been friendly with. There was a lot of partying, heavy drinking, and a great deal of arguing between the couples, including us. I am not using these people as an excuse, but merely as background for my story. I had a choice and I let myself get involved with these people.

My husband, J., and I had not been getting along for over a year. Our relationship was not a happy one. We had talked about counseling but we never got any further than talk. There was no one specific thing that either one of us could say was bothering us, just a constant turmoil. I bitched and nagged at him and he bitched and nagged at me. What a cycle! I know now that these arguments were underlying symptoms of a marriage really gone sour. The heavy drinking and partying only worsened our life. The bickering soon became arguing, the arguing became fighting, and the fighting soon became physical. We were never alone with each other and I don't think either one of us wanted to be. There was always somebody coming or going with a bottle in his hand. The police were called a couple of times to stop wild parties. I found this very embarrassing. I don't think either one of us was ever alcoholic. Neither one of us ever has quit drinking completely. We now have a drink or two before dinner and that is it for the evening. If we are out for the evening, or playing cards, we have a few drinks like everybody else and that is it. Yet neither one of us ever stated that we were going to quit or cut down. That is just the way we are now. There was a time when neither one of us was ever without a glass in his hands.

I had always been very active community-wise and I continued that. I was out about three nights a week for some church, school, or political activity. The weekends were spent with our "friends" in drunken brawls and this was our life. What a waste! Things got worse and worse.

Because of drinking and late hours, I was doing a lousy job at work. I failed to show up for work one day and I was fired — after nine years. I was mortified, but not enough to change. I told all kinds of lies about why I was not working. I know now that God was trying to tell me something. I started collecting unemployment compensation, and pretty soon our life was back to the same old misery.

I began to look for ways to run away — from J., from myself, and from life. I contemplated suicide a few times, but my father's death had been a suicide and that left a mark on me, so I tried killing myself the hard way, by drinking and chasing. I found what I thought was a great way to escape. I had an affair. I chose the scuzziest, bummiest con man that I have ever met to have this great love affair with. When I think about it now, I realize how little I cared about myself. I let myself be seen out in public with this man and I went to motels with him. By this time, his third wife had divorced him, which should have told me something. He kept giving me a snow job about how we were going to get married. I kept telling myself that I was in love with him and that he would make a better husband than J. would. After about a year of this great passion of the century, I told J. that I wanted a divorce so that I could marry the other guy. Everybody in our community knew about the affair except my husband. The husband really was the last to know.

During the year of the affair, I had stood in the center of my living room, stomped my feet, and screamed, "God, get the hell out of my life!" I didn't have to feel guilty if I didn't think God was watching me. What a dummy!

Well, of course, all hell broke loose after my announcement of the affair. The war went on for a week. In the meantime, I was scared. The affair finally ended and J. forgave me, but he could not forget and I can't blame him. Every time we had an argument, my affair got thrown into my face. Our lives became more and more miserable. He didn't want me to leave the house because he was afraid I was going to meet another man. We kept drinking more and more.

Finally, I tried another means of escape. I took money from our savings account, had a girlfriend drive me to the bus station, and bought a ticket for the first bus that was leaving town. The bus happened to be going to H. — a helluva town to be going to in the middle of a Minnesota winter. I rented a furnished apartment, bought dishes and bedding, and moved in. It was also a helluva town to find a job in. I had no entertainment, no TV, very little money left, and didn't know a soul in town. I did some pretty heavy thinking though. After a week I called my girlfriend and found out that J. had not been able to work all week. He had been camped on everybody's doorstep looking for me and was in very bad shape emotionally. I called him and told him to come and get me. To this day I don't know whether it was for his sake or for mine. That week's escape cost us around $500.

Things were better for a time after that. He was glad to have me home and acted like it. I was still unhappy. I had too much time on my hands. I wasn't working and I was ashamed to go any place. I quit all my meetings and simply stayed home, full of self-pity.

My next escape route was a little bit different. We were still drinking pretty heavily and that "old gang" was still hanging around. The girls took me out for lunch on my fortieth birthday which, of course, lasted all afternoon at the restaurant and into the wee hours at our house. I got sick to my stomach and vomited a bucket full of blood. They rushed me to the hospital and, you guessed it, I had an ulcer. They kept me in the hospital for sixteen days. This was another escape. I enjoyed it. I was in a big cocoon, safe from everything, including life. I had a lot of visitors, J. came every night, but I was always glad when they left. I did not want to go home. Everything at the hospital was peaceful and serene. There were no fights. The day came when they told me I was released to go home and take it easy. I took them literally. That's the day I took to the couch and the bed.

This was my new escape from reality. I slept until noon every day and then took my blanket and pillow to the couch. I stayed there every day until two or three in the morning, whatever time the TV went off, and then I took three sleeping pills and went to bed until the next day began all over again. I never did a dish, cooked a meal, made a bed, or got dressed. My husband would come home from work at night trying to be cheerful. He smiled and tried to talk to me a lot. I just didn't have any comments for him. Most of the time I just grunted. He made supper, did the dishes, cleaned the house, and never once tried to get me to do anything. He did try to get me to go to a movie or for a ride or anything to get me out of the house. I would not budge. I think I left that couch only twice in a year and a half, and both outings turned out just as disastrously as I had expected them to. Naturally, that's what I was looking for. I had an excuse to go back to my couch. I knew what was happening to me. I was fully aware of what I was doing to myself. I just plain didn't give a damn! I am certain that I had a nervous breakdown, but it was never diagnosed because I would not go near my doctor. He knew me well enough and I knew him well enough that I knew what he would say to me — "M.J., get up off your duff and do something." I wasn't ready to hear that.

Finally I agreed to help with some Christmas shopping much against my better judgment. We were in a bookstore and I spotted a book called *I Ain't Much, Baby, But I'm All I've Got.* Up until my couch time, I had always been a voracious reader. I usually had three or four books going at the same time. I had not read a thing, not even a newspaper in a year and a half. But the title of this book intrigued me. It was the first thing I had shown any interest in for a long while. I think that was one of J.'s biggest thrills — seeing me buy a book.

Well, you know what happened to me after I read the book. I read about EA and a gong sounded in my head. I immediately went to the phone and found out where the nearest group was meeting. The part that got through to me was the way the author talked about the love in EA groups. Love was the magic word for me. I didn't know how to love or how to accept love.

The first meeting that I went to was a kind of letdown. I passed when it was my turn and just listened. I heard all the talk about God and Higher Power and that threatened me and turned me off. The leader asked if I had any questions and I asked, "What if you don't want to believe in God?" They all smiled at me and told me that I didn't have to if I didn't want to. They didn't react the way I wanted them to. I expected that they would throw me out and tell me not to come back. But they just gave me a cute comeback. I continued going to meetings and trying hard to work the Program. I was still fighting God though. I am so glad that He persisted and finally got through to me, which of course is what I wanted all the time. I had such a hard time admitting I was powerless that the whole group applauded the first time that I said it. I was a fighter, but instinctively — and with the help of my Higher Power — I was fighting to get well.

Eventually, I found a job that I love dearly and where they like me and let me know it. I have improved so much that J. tells everybody all about me. Believe me, I am not anonymous any more. There is still a long way to go. Hopefully, I grow a little every day. The Twelve-Step Program is a daily one. I study the Twelve Steps every day along with meditating. Maybe it is only for a short time, but I do it. I owe my life to EA and I know it! I am so grateful for the things I have learned, the growth I have made, and the friends I have met. I am particularly grateful to the Program for helping me to find my good Friend God again, although I know that He was the one who pushed me into that bookstore.

As I said, I use these Twelve Steps, the Just For Todays, and the Slogans every day. I have learned how to love and to accept love. It is a very slow process but I see the light ahead in the tunnel. I am learning how to cry and, believe me, when you don't know how to cry it can be a tough life. I have sense enough now to really talk to God, to ask for help, and to expect to get it when I really need it the most. I have sense enough now to thank God for all the blessings I have, including a wonderful husband who literally lived with me in hell for many years and still stuck by me. I have learned humility and to appreciate nature. I am not afraid of tomorrow anymore. I am not afraid to die. I am afraid of pain but I'll worry about that when the time comes. I have come a long way from that day when I first lay down on the couch, and it hasn't taken all that long either.

I have worked at this new job for over three years now and I love it. I know that my Higher Power put me there. Hopefully I help people in my work. I work hard but willingly. I appreciate my job and my boss lets me know that he appreciates me. I recently received a reclassification and a promotion that happens only about once in fifty years. That was really a thrill. From a de-activated member of the church, I have become a lector in our parish. Formerly when I did go to church, which was very seldom, I had to sit in the back because I couldn't breathe. Now, as a lector, I sit on the altar. I have once again become active in church work. Among other things, I work on the church paper as an editor and a writer of a monthly column. I go to school once a week simply because I enjoy it. Our marriage isn't perfect yet, but it sure is one helluva lot better. I am not running away from life any more. I am trying to get all the living I can in each day. All of these things have come to me because of EA.

I got rid of all this garbage that I have written about during my first Fifth Step. I had a wonderful and loving counselor who took my written inventory and tore it up and threw it in the fireplace. He burned it and told me that that part of my life was past. I was forgiven and I should forget it forever. Those were the most wonderful words that I have ever heard. I believed him and I still do. I am bringing up the past now just to share my story with you to show you what Twelve, simple but powerful and hard, Steps can do for you. I guess the most important thing I have learned through the Twelve-Step EA Program is that life is worth living. It is wonderful to be alive. For that knowledge, I thank EA and all of the wonderful members of that group.

Mary Jane

(22)

NO MORE PAST AND FUTURE — JUST TODAY

My name is John and I have emotional problems. This is my story, written not because it is unique, but rather in the hope that it might be similar to that of persons reading it and offer hope to them.

It took me a long time to come to the point where I could make the simple statement, "I have emotional problems." I was taught to make that statement by members of Emotions Anonymous or "EA" as it is known by members. This is a success story for EA, since I feel I owe my life and present sanity to the organization and its precepts and program. It is also a story of how the Program continues to help me retain sanity since my emotional problem is not cured but rather only controlled.

My major symptom of emotional illness took the form of depression which is apparently the most common of mental illnesses. In my case, the depression was and is the result of many other complex and interrelated emotions and emotional problems.

I feel that they are directly related to my rearing, training and the environment in which I lived. I am not blaming my parents, community, school, or the American way of life. I am suggesting that these do create pressures with which many have not yet learned to cope. The result is emotional problems. My story can perhaps then be summed up as a story of how one man was forced to learn to cope.

I grew up on a farm in the Midwest. Looking back, I would rank it as a typical middle class rural background.

Our family was probably above average. My mother was college-educated as a teacher. My father was a very self-sufficient and progressive farmer.

I feel that my emotional problems started and were reinforced at an early age. I can't really identify any specific thing to blame them on. I call them the result of a "way of life." In my case, they are the result of being taught to have expectations and live in the future rather than the present. I was also taught by example to repress and not show emotion. The result was frustration and depression.

I think my youth can be summed up as trying to be the best in everything. I tried hard and was not satisfied with any achievement I made. For example, I graduated at the top of my high school class but wasn't satisfied because it was a small class. I was on the student council for three years and active in many activities. Yet I didn't feel I was really accepted.

I went on to college because it was expected of me. Here I had my first real experience with failure and my first signs of emotional illness.

After two years of college, I found that I couldn't handle the math required in my chosen field. By this time I had married, mainly I think, because I wasn't certain of my capability to attract a girl other than my teenage steady or to take care of myself.

Finding that I couldn't count on my well laid-out future was a real shock. I experienced my first mild case of depression. However, I was still young and flexible enough to be able to switch my goals and begin to plan a new future around a different career.

I graduated from college and obtained an excellent job. By now I had learned that I might not be able to be "tops" in everything I tried. I thus learned a new way to avoid living in the present. I learned to live in the past and beat myself mentally for not doing better or not making a different decision. Thus I was making unobtainable plans and then worrying about my stupidity and laziness since I hadn't achieved the plans. To complicate things, my plans were not solid, and they changed. I didn't know what it would take to make me happy. I just knew it was something different, in the future, and hadn't been achieved.

After three years I decided I should change jobs to advance my career. I think the only reason I wanted to advance was that it was the "expected" thing.

The new job was a manager's job, and I soon was expecting so much of myself and had so many problems both real and imagined that I began to have my first really serious mental breakdown. I became non-functional on the job and unable to think clearly or handle many simple tasks. I saw a doctor who gave me drugs and counseling. At the time I didn't really know how sick I was.

I was able to change jobs again. I was able to leave an intolerable situation and begin a new round of planning a future to avoid living the present.

Things went well on the new job. My family grew to five children. A few times I almost accepted myself and began to live in the present. At times I was even happy. I feared happiness and somehow felt I was letting people down. I would soon be off chasing the next advancement rainbow or feeling sorry for my mistakes and imagined failures, since things were stable.

At age thirty-five my failure to live in the present finally caught up with me. By this time I had realized some of my planned future. I had an excellent well-paying job, a wonderful family, and an acreage in the country. Still I couldn't be happy or accept it. I just didn't know how to live in the present.

I felt completely frustrated. I had done what was expected in achieving the good life. However, it didn't make me happy and I no longer had a dream to chase. I considered myself a middle-aged failure.

I threw myself into my job and other activities to try to avoid the thoughts and unhappiness. It didn't help and made matters worse since I began to physically exhaust myself and set myself up for failure since it was impossible to achieve my plans. I reached a point where I could no longer function in my job. I can remember sitting at my desk for hours trying to look busy and not being able to think clearly or perform the simplest tasks.

My job involved travel so I began to travel excessively to a plant where we were having severe problems. For awhile, I hid by traveling to handle some simple job which could have been better handled by phone or memo.

My nervous breakdown came to a head when I became completely non-functional while traveling. I wasn't even able to make airline reservations for the return trip. This was something that I had done hundreds of times during my career. When I was sent home, I was hospitalized against my will. I refused to admit that I was ill.

I embarked on a series of hospitalizations, drugs and shock treatments. I was able at times to "con" my way out of the hospital by acting "normal" and giving the proper answers to questions. This went on over three or four months. I hated being confined but still refused to admit that I was ill. My condition worsened in spite of the drugs and other treatment. This was, I now feel, because I refused to admit my illness.

Twice I attempted to take my life. Then my local doctors gave up on me and shipped me off to the University of Minnesota Hospital. This was considered a last resort. Prior to this change of hospitals, my wife found the support of the local Emotions Anonymous group. In fact, I attended a few meetings with her while out of the hospital.

While in the University Hospital, I learned of the power of the EA Program. First I began to get calls and visits from EA members. Their message was simple. They said, "We've been where you are and recovered. We care." For someone who refuses to even face their illness because it is so frightening, these are the most important words he can hear. Others have emotional problems and have learned to live with them. Recovery and return to normalcy is possible.

In addition to the support of EA members, my recovery was made possible by my first admission of illness. I also began to take an interest in and try to help some of my fellow patients as part of the EA Program. I was given lithium salt treatment which has shown excellent results for treatment of depression. I feel that each thing supported the other and recovery would not have been possible without all.

To make a long story short, I was released in less than six weeks, and then completely off drugs and treatment in four months. During this period I worked as hard as possible at the EA Program, attending as many as five meetings a week, going to retreats, speaking at meetings and so on. To put things in perspective, it should be noted that when I was at the University Hospital, it was the doctors' opinion that there was a chance of my being hospitalized for the rest of my life. When released, I was told that I would most likely need drug treatment the rest of my life. As a result of EA, I have lived with my emotional problems and remained sane for three years without drugs or other treatment. I could not have done this without EA.

My problems did not go away; I learned to deal with them. My original illness came from my inability to accept myself and live in the present. There was no identifiable crisis in my life as often causes severe emotional illness. I have since had to deal with some very real problems. I was faced with the fact that my wife found another man, and divorced me. With the help of EA and its members, I was able to survive.

I did learn that the Program must be practiced in total to work well. I learned the importance of the Fifth Step, admitting faults to God and a counselor. I learned the importance of forgiving and accepting that which cannot be changed. EA is a program which works only as well as one works the Program.

As with many EA members, I feel I owe my life and sanity to the EA Twelve-Step Program. I know my story is not unique or awe-inspiring. It is my hope and prayer that those who read it may find hope, and in time, the serenity I have as a result of this Program.

John

(23)
I'M NOT HERE BECAUSE I NEED HELP

I don't know if my story will help anyone, but by writing it, it will have helped at least one person — me. I hope along the way maybe a word or phrase will help someone else too, the way others' stories have given me strength.

I came to EA in a pretty mixed-up state of mind. I'd heard there was some help awaiting me in the Twelve-Step Program, but I felt I wasn't "that bad off yet" to need a Program of this sort. So I proceeded to procrastinate until I got myself "that bad off." I had nothing to lose because I was so unhappy and miserable. Besides, I thought, I won't tell anyone I'm going to an EA meeting.

Well, I waited until I was alone and feeling pretty lousy and finally called for a list of the meetings, times, and places and found one nearby. I went, and for the first few weeks played the "I'm not here because I need help" game. Naturally I wasn't getting well because I wasn't being honest with myself or my group. With the help of group members' talks, I finally decided to risk telling a few things.

No one even flinched. This led me to dare to tell more and more and more, as I sensed the group's acceptance of all my weaknesses. I dared to tell them I was afraid my husband would fall out of love with me and leave. I dared to tell them I was afraid of people's criticism. I even dared to say I wanted to be all alone where no one could hurt me. I didn't want love or favors or anything because I feared that those giving these things would ask something back. I wanted to be selfish and not give anything of myself to anyone. Well, after several meetings when I had told all these things and no one kicked me out, I was amazed. I was so used to pretending I was whoever I was supposed to be with whomever I was with, that I couldn't believe that these people didn't object to my being me. What a feeling!

Now I was beginning to grasp the EA Program and I was able to begin the Steps. First I admitted powerlessness over my emotions and then owned up to my insane attitudes.

When I got to my Fourth Step I decided to really let it all hang out and did what I thought was a pretty honest inventory. The only problem was that I only touched briefly on what I later learned was a very big part of my self-hatred and desire to be away from people. I was forty-five pounds overweight and had always been a fat person, up to seventy-six pounds overweight at one time. I had rationalized that if people didn't like me because I was fat I didn't need them or anyone. What I forgot was that my fatness was *my* excuse for being a crummy person and people shied away because of my bad behavior and cutting tongue, not my fat.

I was fortunate in having a very perceptive counselor when I took my Fifth Step, and he saw my problem and very kindly helped me see it. At first I was hostile when he so casually told me one of my biggest problems was lack of self-esteem and self-worth and that the underlying reasons were directly related to my weight. He said, "If you *really* wanted to be thin, you'd be thin." I had heard these words before but with God's help and EA growth, all of a sudden they said more to me. I actually had the choice. I'd always accepted my fatness as my fate in life, and what I tried to pretend was unimportant.

I left the counselor's office feeling very optimistic and my emotions felt great. I had been given hope of normalcy! I began to pray for strength, something EA taught me God would do for me, and amazingly I heard of a doctor whose diet sounded as if I could handle it. With a lot of praying and work I lost my weight and am at present a trim 120 pounds, and it's wonderful how many of my other problems melted away with the fat.

I still have many emotional problems, however, and need the support of EA to help me through bad times. All my attitudes are changing through the help and grace of God and the support of EA and my group. Without all these things, I'd probably get fat and miserable again, turning to food to cover up the problems which arise in daily living. I can choose to use my Program and prayer instead of eating. I need EA more than ever now and it's always there. It is a beautiful Program and a wonderful new way of life. The answers are all there.

Emotions Anonymous gave me the tools to find my self-esteem and self-respect. I can look in a mirror and smile at what I see; I can look at people and my family and friends and trust them not to hurt me. I can share myself and give of myself without fearing rejection. These lovely new feelings allow me to be a better person, which in turn reinforces my self-esteem. I finally have the wheel going in a positive direction. Before EA it only went backward into negativeness and feelings of self-contempt.

Whatever your troubles are, however similar or dissimilar to mine, the answer to a happier life lies in the Twelve Steps of our Program. These steps introduce us to a Power greater than anything — God is there to help you. He is your friend and constant companion if you'll only ask Him to walk with you as He has with me. I pray I'll continue to daily ask Him to be my guide and source of hope and strength.

Thank you, EA, for introducing me to my best Friend.

Anonymous

(24)
A NORMAL STORY

I need the Twelve Step Program of EA in order to live a new way of life. It took many years of "normal" living before I finally realized, admitted, and accepted the fact that I had emotional problems and needed help. I had good parents, had been raised in a stable home, had attended church and Sunday School, had participated in sports and other extra-curricular activities, got good grades in school (graduated valedictorian of my high school class, honors in college, number one in my class in the seminary).

I am thirty-nine years old, have been married for seventeen years, have three lovely daughters, eight, twelve, and fourteen, and am a Lutheran minister. As a minister I was the pastor of a rural Wisconsin parish for three years, was a hospital psychiatric chaplain for seven years and have been a chaplain in an alcoholism and drug treatment center for two years.

I have never had a nervous breakdown and have not been hospitalized for mental or emotional illness and problems. Yet I know that I have problems with my emotions, and that coming to my EA meetings and living the EA Program is changing me. I am now happier, more confident, and more believing and trusting in God as my Higher Power in a daily and more practical way then I ever was before.

What made me realize that I had emotional problems and needed help? What led me into EA? There are two specific things: an ulcer on my vocal chords in 1969 that was related to anxiety, stress and work (and I was a preacher!) and exposure to recovering alcoholics and the AA Program. This exposure began as part of my chaplaincy work in 1971.

These two specific things in my life began to help me get the message that something was wrong with me. I was suffering more feelings of stress, anxiety, tension and depression than was good for me and I knew I had better do something to take care of myself if I wasn't going to die young of throat cancer or a heart attack!

I was attracted by the recovering AA's I met and felt they had something I didn't have but I wanted. They seemed to me to be people who were mature, realistic, happy, confident, loving, giving, receiving, and depending upon a personal spiritual relationship with God as they understood Him, as their source of strength and life. They had the Twelve Step Program of AA as a way of life. But I wasn't an alcoholic!

I joined EA in the summer of 1974. When I first learned of the existence of Emotions Anonymous, I knew it was what I had been looking for and what I needed. I have learned a lot about myself in EA and I have found that the concepts, slogans, steps and fellowship of the Program work. They are helping me to grow, to change, and to live a new way of life.

I can now see that many negative emotions and negative emotional reactions were troubling me and causing me problems throughout my life. I can see that fear has troubled me all of my life — fear of failure and fear of people. When my dad came to watch me play baseball, I would strike out. When I felt under pressure in a football game I would drop the ball. I can see that my needs for approval were so strong they were hurting me. I can see that I suffered from depression when in college and seminary. My perfectionism, fear, and lack of self-confidence made vocational choosing a painful struggle for me during those years. I have always had difficulty making decisions, big ones or little ones, which are evidence of my fear and perfectionism. I can see that I developed unhealthy (I like to say "neurotic") emotional patterns, such as becoming anxious, uptight, depressed or having physical symptoms such as cold hands, tics in my eyes or nose and eventually, the ulcer in my throat. I can see that I developed patterns of negative thinking such as expecting failure, looking for the bad, worrying, being critical and judgmental of myself, my wife and children. I also knew all along that I felt a certain sense of loneliness and wished for deeper friendships.

I now know that my main personal defects are my self-centeredness and my pride, and they led me into a lot of fear and perfectionistic needs to control. I have suffered a lot of emotional frustration and pain from it. I do believe in God, but my self-centeredness has and does prevent me from depending on and trusting in God in a real sense. I want God, yet I want to run my own show; I want to be God myself.

I thank God now for the EA Program. It is helping me live more comfortably, happily, and realistically. It is helping me be a better husband and father. I thank God I found EA while my children are as young as they are. I am learning to "let go" with my wife and daughters. I am learning to "live and let live." I am learning to live with real faith, trust, and dependency on God so it is helping me be a better pastor. The whole thing for me has been a slow, gradual process. I haven't experienced any miraculous changes or conversion, but I do feel and know that I am now beginning to learn to live as a human being - even though I am a minister and even though others may have looked at my thirty-six years of life before I got into EA and may have judged me to be a normal and successful person. After all, I didn't see my own need for help for a long time. I believe that by the grace of God I am in EA now.

Ron

(25)

NO MORE TRANQUILIZERS

My interest in good emotional health began in 1949 following a severe nervous breakdown. I had to be placed in the psychiatric ward of a hospital and was given twelve electric shock treatments in addition to other therapy.

I feel quite lucky in that I was only off work about two and one-half months, returning to my same job, performing it satisfactorily even though I had been facing dismissal before I had the breakdown.

Everything I read about manic depressives indicated I would probably have to be hospitalized several times during my life and have more shock treatments. I certainly did not look forward to that and made up my mind I was going to stay as emotionally and mentally healthy as possible.

One thing I learned early was that when I talked with people who were having mental, nervous, or emotional problems and tried to encourage them by telling them quite candidly what had happened to me, I began to feel better, especially if I felt I could help them over some of the rough spots on their road to recovery. From time to time my psychiatrist had referred patients to me who were interested in knowing someone who had survived a nervous breakdown. I was still struggling hard, but in helping someone else, I managed to put on a brave front and it became easier for me and the struggle less. I was doing Twelfth Step work then, but did not realize it.

In 1954 I married. My husband and I moved hundreds of miles away and lived on an air base for two years.

I worked temporarily for a surgeon as a secretary-nursing assistant. I had not told the doctor of my breakdown as I knew I would not have been hired if I had. I loved the work even if I did have to pop a tranquilizer in my mouth every time I heard the doctor's car door shut.

It was at this time I began gaining weight from overeating. I could certainly have used an EA group then.

My husband applied for an overseas assignment and was accepted, but I was not allowed to accompany him. I moved back to the hometown and my former job. Then my husband wrote that he had secured housing for us and I was to come to Taiwan.

Just in case I would need tranquilizers, I asked my psychiatrist to write out a prescription for me.

My life in Taipei, Taiwan (Formosa or Free China) was interesting and exciting. I managed to do without tranquilizers until we went to Hong Kong where I was able to purchase some "over the counter." Yes, I had to start taking some before we came back home.

We returned to the States in 1961. My husband had retired from the Air Force. We began to run out of money before his checks started coming, but I was able to get my old job back. In fact, they gave me two raises as they had carried me on leave of absence.

It was rough trying to work eight hours a day, five and a half days a week in addition to cooking and cleaning a furnished apartment which I hated.

My work became increasingly harder. Several employees were jealous of my having been given leaves of absence. My boss suggested several times that I take an extra long lunch hour to take care of business. However, another man was soon put in charge of our department. He increased my work and I kept getting further behind. When I tried to talk to him, his only comment was, "We will just have to knuckle down and work harder."

Because we needed the money, there was only one thing left for me to do. I went back to my psychiatrist and he put me on tranquilizers.

A few years later, my mother fell and broke her hip. I had been fighting the battle of the bulge successfully as I had to do all my life, and managed to stay on my diet until the day my mother was buried. Then I began eating constantly. I also developed terrible abdominal cramps. After seeing several doctors, I finally returned to my psychiatrist who suggested I be hospitalized for tests, but that I enter the psychiatric ward in case it was my nerves. I agreed.

I stayed at the hospital three weeks but went home on weekends. They found no physical condition to cause my trouble. The psychiatrist changed the tranquilizers and after a few weeks my trouble cleared up.

The next few years became nightmares. A month after my husband and I had spent a wonderful Christmas in Hawaii, my younger brother, to whom I was very close, was hospitalized. The doctors found nothing and were going to send him home.

I was alone when the phone rang; it was my sister saying my brother was in serious condition. I remember running around the house and screaming and crying. Finally I pulled myself together enough to telephone my psychiatrist to ask how many tranquilizers I could safely take in a twenty-four hour period. He said six, and I stayed on these six tranquilizers a day until I heard of EA.

By taking a leave of absence from my job, I spent as much time at the hospital as possible, driving back and forth after taking tranquilizers. My brother died within the year.

It was at my brother's funeral in November of 1973 that I learned my aunt was given six months to live, due to cancer. Together with my brother and sister, I spent the weekends of the next six months taking turns caring for her and her husband.

About this time I saw my psychiatrist and told him how depressed I was and that I would like to retire. He said I should not. Three months later, he suggested I go back into the hospital psychiatric ward for depression. I readily agreed and stayed three weeks. He advised me to take an early disability retirement. I was beginning to feel as I had in 1949, having dizzy spells. My psychiatrist explained the dizzy spells were due to my dreading having to go back to work, and he was right! I consulted another psychiatrist who also said I should retire.

It was now 1974 and I read about Emotions Anonymous. I was familiar with the Twelve-Step Program. I thought, "This is what I was looking for in 1949." I wrote immediately for more information and knew I would start an EA group here. In 1949 I was looking for something so I could help others. This time I had found something to help myself as well as others.

After attending the EA Annual Roundup in St. Paul in October of 1974, I came back home and started the first EA group here. In 1975 I was overjoyed when one of our members said she wanted to start a night group. I told her I would be glad to help the group get started, but that I did not want the full responsibility of another group. I attend two EA meetings whenever possible each week and always attend at least one.

After I had been in EA for several months I kept wondering when I would have my spiritual awakening. I was doing Twelfth Step work, but I thought I should have had a spiritual awakening. Then I realized that for me it had been something that came on gradually. I didn't see stars or hear bells ringing, but I had a peace of mind, a serenity and happiness such as I had never had before.

Then and there I decided I should cut down on tranquilizers. My psychiatrist suggested I cut down from the six to five for a month and then to four and so forth. Now I'm down to zilch! The day of my uncle's funeral I took one just in case, and the day I had to go to Probate Court during a tornado watch I took one, but with the help of EA I feel I have kicked the habit!

All the days are not perfect for me, but EA has helped me get through some trying situations, such as when it was suspected I had cancer, or when my husband mows both the grass and my flowers.

Even with the problems I had last year, I saw my psychiatrist only twice, once in January when his secretary said he had to see me about some papers, and in December when I thought I had cancer.

My Higher Power willing, I plan to attend EA every week as long as I live. I feel I owe my sanity to EA and I try to carry the message whenever I have the opportunity.

Marge

(26)

THEY REFUNDED MY MISERIES

My first encounter with EA was three years ago. I heard one of the members give a talk about it at one of our church meetings. I went to three or four meetings and then stopped going. I guess I hadn't hit bottom yet. I had gotten enough from those few meeting for what I needed at that particular time.

A year later I hit rock bottom. Although I had never been hospitalized or had a breakdown I was really hurting. I couldn't think straight, my mind and vision were a blur, and my reactions to circumstances and people were totally irrational.

I thought I was going crazy. I screamed at everyone all the time and my language would have shocked a truck driver. At times I hit my kids for no reason at all and always had a guilty feeling afterward. I'd see them so hurt by my irrational behavior and I'd feel so helpless and alone when it was all over. My fights with my husband were a daily routine too.

I would spend hours trying to decide what blouse to wear and peeling a potato was more than I could bear. The decision of whether to cook hamburgers or hot dogs blew my mind. I slept a lot daytimes, hardly at all nights. If I wasn't worried about the future, I was turning the past over and over in my mind. I always worried about what I said to other people, what they thought of me. I felt there had to be some other way for me to handle things, but I didn't know how.

One Saturday, after one of my "crazies," I knew I had

211

hit bottom and if I didn't get help right then and there, I had had it. I can remember asking God to please help me know what to do to help myself, to please never let me get any worse than I was then. With that prayer came a thought about EA. I remembered those few meetings and I felt I at least had somewhere to go. I put on my coat and told my husband to watch the kids because I was going to an EA meeting. I remember being so scared I could hardly see and I shook so much I could hardly talk. My heart felt like it was going to thump right out of my chest.

At the meeting I was welcomed by everyone and the love and acceptance was beautiful. Some even remembered me from the previous year and that still amazes me. After I told my tale of woe I found they hadn't heard anything shocking or unique and they still accepted me. They told me to come back and give them a chance. That was two years ago. I am still in EA and always will be.

EA has taught me the difference between symptoms and causes. It has taught me about my emotions and what to do with them and that emotions are okay. It's taught me to try and solve my problems instead of running away from them. If there is no solution here and now, I have learned to be patient, trust in God and myself, and there will be a solution when I am ready for it. Since being in EA I no longer shake. My thinking has cleared and my vision is no longer blurred. Almost all of my anxieties are gone, along with many of my other symptoms. I am more open to people now so they can see the real me. I don't worry so much any more about what they think of me because I know I'm a pretty neat gal.

I have lost much of my fear, and the fear has been replaced by confidence, both in myself and my Higher Power. I had lost all contact with God and EA showed me how to find Him again. I now know Him as a friend and protector for both me and my family, and I feel a warm closeness with Him.

I do not procrastinate as much as I used to, I'm willing to admit when I have made a mistake, and it is easier for me to say I'm sorry.

Although I am still into my self-centeredness, I am able to honestly care and feel love for other people. EA has taught me to be honest with myself and others and how to live with myself and others. EA doesn't solve my problems for me — it teaches me to solve them for myself or to at least cope with them if there is no solution yet. I have made many beautiful and loving friends in EA these past two years and the best friend I made is my God. I have gone back to school and am taking on new challenges I never dreamed I'd ever try, much less succeed at.

I have survived through a move to another state, and starting a new EA group there. I couldn't have done it without the EA tools which taught me how to live a new way of life. I am very grateful for the Program, for my new-found friends, and to my new-found friend, God, for being so patient with me. I still have a long way to go yet but I am better than I was and EA and God will help me to continue to grow in my new way of life.

Madeline

(27)
THE GEOGRAPHICAL CURE

I was born in early winter of 1940. Grown to age seven with Dad often gone, I recall my first years as pretty normal, happy, and yet confusing. Dad was in the service and those brief furloughs seemed filled with drinking and arguments that I only absorbed as confusion.

At age eight we moved to a small town and I was strongly turned on to religion. After I graduated from eighth grade, I convinced my folks that I wanted to be a nun and away I went to the convent. In those years I already compared myself to everyone I knew and always came out on the bottom. Now I realize that my search for a perfect life led me to the convent, a search which was to be filled with mental and emotional illness.

I was always full of feeling — "high-strung," Mom said. I once beat up a neighbor girl in a fit of rage. I can still hear her head bump as I hit her to the ground again and again. Only later did I realize that I was fighting with a girl considered "good" by my friends. That pattern of dishonest anger has traveled with me many a year and only now does awareness help change it.

The convent years were happy and inspiring. The only problems that developed from it were a scrupulous mind, and an inability to make my own decisions because obedience was a safer, easier way. So by the time I was finished with high school and ready for the novitiate, I was so full of fear and anxiety that I couldn't sleep nights. I was hospitalized at the convent and later sent home where my family put me into a "psych" ward in my home town.

214

I was afraid of myself, afraid of failure, afraid of sex, and afraid of men. I was put into "lockup" and later treated with medical therapy. With a little psychiatric counseling, I went home with pills and a promise to return periodically for refills.

I wanted to succeed at something and school was easy for me so I went to college. In the university setting I had many decisions which I was afraid to make and little ability to develop friends. Thus after a year and a half I was ready to marry the first boyfriend who liked me. I could not be honest enough to admit I didn't love him, and again I started severe insomnia and irrational thinking to take away the decision I faced. I was hospitalized again.

After release this time, I again had pills in hand, but no tools to deal with my feelings. I felt very dissatisfied with myself. I worked in a factory and started dating. Everyone I met seemed not good enough for me. I finally moved and got a teaching job in a bigger city. I was still very active in a religious young people's group and was always looking for the perfect mate. The teaching job was a chance to be a "Savior" and I just immersed myself in it. Soon, exhausted and frightened, I became unable to cope, and with severe insomnia and more irrational thinking, I was again hospitalized. This time I also had met the perfect mate and I didn't even know how to be a friend to him.

My stay in the hospital was shorter this time, and my perfect mate became a faithful pen pal for the next ten years. Later I did marry him, but before I could ever face that, I decided I was going into psychotherapy to be able to deal with my illnesses. In four years of bi-weekly sessions at thirty-five dollars each I began to understand my lack of identity and confidence. I also found out how little trust I had in any other person. I did set up a goal to finish college and to become a certified teacher. I also fell in love with my doctor. I gained few of the necessary principles I needed for daily life. I did start to reach out to men and this was very difficult for me.

After graduation from college, I met and dated a divorced man. It was my first break from my ultra religious practices of the past. I really wanted to share bed and bread with him, but I didn't have the guts. Instead, in my dishonest way, I said goodbye to him and went on a luxury tour of the East. On the tour I transferred all my affection to the tour guide who glady shared his bed with me. It seemed a way for me to prove how unsuccessful and no good I was. After the tour I went back to the psychiatrist. Now I had a real double life — my "good" life of a teacher and my "no good" life with men. I had three other affairs which gave me some feelings of acceptance and I used all of it as proof of my horribleness.

At age twenty-nine I finally decided to go to the town where my faithful pen pal lived. Over the years we had become open friends through our letters and after four months of sharing bread, not bed, we were married. I felt as if I had reached an impossible goal and now I was going to be the perfect wife and mother, no matter how dishonest I had to be.

It didn't work. After I became pregnant, we went into a counseling group. It was helpful and we lived through the first three years with only occasional upheavals. I had started to become honest. It was hard. Then our second girl was born and I became so afraid of a third pregnancy that I flipped out again. I began the insomnia along with wild ideas and plans of ways I would be famous and worthwhile. I ended this in the hospital again. With pills I was brought under control and back to face the world, but I needed more help. It was at this point that I found Emotions Anonymous and reluctantly attended. For six months I fought the Program, analyzed it, blamed it for its lack of immediate results, and then I finally accepted it. I dug in and started to see fruit.

While searching to replace the pills, I found a doctor who diagnosed me as hypoglycemic with low blood sugar. I started a diet of no sugar or caffeine. With the help of the Program I kept this diet, a thing I never could have done in the past. I continued to go to weekly meetings and slowly I began to understand the reality of serenity.

After two years in EA I feel it has taught me about meaningful living. I am finally human and acceptable to myself. I have a program of action that takes work, but it gives results. I am filled with awareness and acceptance of my needs and now I am learning more about the action necessary for serenity. It is wonderful. One of my favorite Just For Today's is, "I will be unafraid to be happy, to enjoy what is good and lovely in life." I feel like the song, "It's a long, long road to freedom — but when you walk in love with the wind on your wings and cover the earth with the songs you sing, the miles fly by." Emotions Anonymous teaches me the songs to sing.

Barb

(28)

INTO THE LAP OF GOD

I was born and raised in a quiet suburb of Boston, Massachusetts, along with a younger brother and an older sister. My father was a good-looking Irishman, quiet and small in stature. My mother was English and always appeared to have a weight problem which she was constantly battling. There was little physical contact and no expression of feelings.

When I was six years old I lighted a match to the hem of my dress. Although I do not remember striking the match or any part of the general scene, I do remember the terror I felt when my mother threw me to the ground in an attempt to extinguish the flames. She slapped the fire out with her hands. In my child's mind I believed I was being punished for playing with matches. Bits and pieces of the following months are all I can remember of that time. I received third degree burns over half of my body and have used the remaining scars as a means of denying my physical beauty for a good portion of my life. This was to be my first conscious experience in blocking my mind from pain — something which was to become a long-term source of difficulty.

I encountered a constant barrage of "don'ts" and "no's" which made me inhibited throughout my school years. Coming from a strict family hampered my social life, dating, and friends. Although a fair student, I went through school in much of an emotional haze. This too I shut off, denied, and so started closing off self-awareness. I do not recall much of those growing-up years. My self-contempt replaced my self-worth. It was my way of saying that I WAS important; I must be so important that I'm worth condemning; if I were not so bad, everyone would love me. I began to commit psychological suicide. The pain was too unbearable and I chose to die and I retreated into myself.

When I married my first husband, it was to get away from home. I was unprepared for life since I was still mentally and emotionally immature at the age of eighteen. I convinced myself he was the immature mate and divorced him less than a year later.

Throughout the next fifteen guilt-ridden years I went from one marriage to the next trying desperately to find myself, to find what happiness I knew was out there. I took in many people who were in need and gave until I was emotionally drained, financially in the red, and wondering why I still felt empty inside. Along the way I met many fine men but always sabotaged the relationships with my continual questions: "What did he want from me? Do I deserve this nice guy? Will he feed my sick need to control?"

I was always doing something for other people, searching for happiness and peace of mind. I allowed myself to be used as a doormat, a nurse, a bill-payer, a rescuer, a "fix-it," a taxi driver, and whatever else anyone would ask of me. To preserve myself as a commodity, I bought gifts continuously for others' praise and attention so I would not feel worthless. I would do anything I could to get people to like me, but the more I did, the more I was used. I hated myself for not being able to be independent of them and for prostituting my feelings. Slowly I became bitter, hard, and more sealed off from my feelings. I felt insignificant and powerless but did not know who the enemy was.

I married men that were as emotionally sick as I, who needed fixing, men I thought would fill all my needs. I was sure I could mold them into men instead of the children I thought them to be. I managed the money, told them where I thought they were wrong, reminded them of their character defects and errors, told them how and when to speak, and bombarded them with my fifty-dollar words to keep them feeling inferior. I taught them how to eat correctly. I needed them to be incapable of functioning independently. They did not know that my self-importance and conceit were signs of inner emptiness, anxiety, and self-doubt.

In return, they resented my, cheated on me, felt threatened by me, dealt out physical abuse, and even hated me. One thing they did not do was leave me. A sick love was better than no love at all. I made them dependent upon me and guilt prevented them from leaving their "mother." After all, wasn't I being the ideal wife and mother? Wasn't I a good housekeeper with everything in its place? Weren't all meals on the table at the exact hour? Didn't I handle everything?

Meanwhile I was feeling agonizingly empty inside. Although I was love-starved, I camouflaged it. They were just as love-starved, but I didn't know how to respond to them or their needs. How could I? I did not know myself how to put my feelings first. I could not verbally express my feelings. I withdrew my affection, then my sexual desires turned to disgust, and the real arguments began.

I learned quite young how to repress my feelings and push down the anger and frustrations I felt. I would not admit defeat. I did not know then that sick people married sick people. I later learned that by keeping them defensive, I didn't have to look at my own character defects.

I was derailed from my emotionally-sick track in the fall of 1974 when I realized that I needed help. I played sick games with four psychiatrists before I found one I could not out-talk, out-maneuver, and out-think. During the time I was seeing these psychiatrists, I was wetting the bed periodically, had severe headaches, anxiety, tension, and shook internally and externally. After I began a comfortable recovery, one of the four psychiatrists said, "I didn't believe you could recover." My mind said nothing was wrong, but my body was telling the truth. Psychosomatic ailments showed that my body and mind were working against each other. I was extremely divorced from my feelings. I was given uppers by day, downers by night, and could have become addicted to the cover-up drugs.

When my current husband returned to California, we made another attempt to make our marriage work. After admitting his alcoholism to himself, he began attending Alcoholics Anonymous on a regular basis. I attended these meetings with him in my attempt to help him, and to know everything he was doing, but soon identified with some of the underlying problems I heard in these meetings.

Although I found I did not have a problem with alcohol, I did have the desire to stop drinking. I had not hit bottom yet, but I believed I might be a potential alcoholic.

While attending a meeting, I heard of Emotions Anonymous and asked for information on a local chapter so that I could attend. There was no information available, nor was there a local meeting.

A friend gave me a book by Jess Lair a short time later which mentioned Emotions Anonymous, along with the address of the central office. I corresponded with them and soon received permission to start a chapter here in the San Diego area. After a few meetings of trial and error, I began to change. My personal growth came in leaps and bounds when I found others reaching out for help for the same reasons I was. I thought I was unique in my emotional hell and that my God had deserted me. Soon I no longer needed to see my psychiatrist.

When I started growing, I began to experience aliveness and wanted to be more informed. I bought every book and raided every library for anything that had to do with psychology, psychiatry, human behavior, self-awareness, assertiveness. I absorbed everything like a sponge and even took psychology in college. Soon I thought I knew enough about human behavior to be able to psychoanalyze anyone I came in contact with. People began avoiding me; I was driving them absolutely crazy. I wanted to help the human race, to make them all emotionally well and stop all wars. . .if only they would listen to me! I forgot Emotions Anonymous was not for people who needed it, but for people who wanted it, and that I could not give away what I didn't have.

Disciplining myself is very difficult when I see someone who is hurting. Carrying the message held more of a responsibility than I had realized. I poured affection on people to the point of obsession. I could not be their psychiatrist nor my own.

Today through Emotions Anonymous I am living a more feeling life. I am getting in touch with the real me that I have strangled and suffocated all these years. I am taking control of my own life and emotions. I find my awarenesses occur when I'm quiet with myself and receptive. Although I had a great sense of tragedy over the loss of my childhood and still do not remember too much about it, it is no longer important. My Higher Power will give that to me when I am ready. I allow others the responsibility for their actions and feelings and have taken full responsibility for my own actions and feelings. I can no longer blame people, places, or things for my behavior.

Now I can trust my expression of affection toward others because it comes from my heart and not my head. Now I know that loving myself is the prerequisite to loving others genuinely. I may marry again, but this time I will know why. I have a lot more to learn about myself and am very anxious to learn. With my Higher Power guiding me, I feel confident that serenity, honest humility, and love of self will accompany me through any storm. I no longer shadow-box with the horrors from the past. I found Emotions Anonymous could not open the doors to heaven and let me in, but it did open the doors to hell and let me out. . .into the lap of God.

Bobbie

(29)

COMPULSIONS

My name is Diane and I am powerless over my emotions. I came into the Emotions Anonymous Program because my life was unmanageable. I had very little concern for myself, for my needs — physical, mental, or emotional. I had no confidence and less self-worth. I could think of no reason for living, for continuing the struggles of daily life.

I have wondered when my emotional problems first began. I know definitely that since the age of sixteen I have done very little sane or rational thinking and acting, but it seemed quite strange to me that up until that time I was supposedly "normal " and then almost overnight became so deluded in my thinking. Recently my mother told me a story about myself. When I was a young child, I used to stand outside of our home waiting for the paper boy to come by and when he did, he would hit me over the head with a paper as he rode by. At first I thought this was just a story about my growing up. Then it dawned on me — what in hell was wrong with me that I continually accepted that kind of treatment? Even at that early age, I must have had very little self-worth to feel that I needed to be hit over the head as a sign of attention and someone caring about me.

I remember little else of my emotional state during childhood except my self-pity and the fears about the changing living situations in my life, my belief that I was always right, my always being a follower and never a leader, my terrible loneliness, my willingness to allow anyone to do almost anything that they wanted to me, and my running away from almost all situations instead of trying to work through any problems. This behavior and these attitudes of mine were excellent training for larger problems which could be seen by almost everyone around me, but which I would not admit to for the next fifteen years.

When I was sixteen, my family moved out of the state because of my father's work. I resented my parents for this move, using the excuse that I could never make new friends and indulged myself in self-pity about leaving the old ones. Instead of admitting to myself and them how scared I was about that move and how painful it was for me, I pretended that the change was exciting.

Because of my resentment, I quit talking to my parents about myself, became depressed, and started believing that they were out to ruin my life. They became quite frustrated by my behavior, so they suggested that I see a psychiatrist. That was the biggest shock of my entire life. I became terribly afraid that I was crazy. I began having some physical problems. My vision became quite blurry; I would be in familiar places and not recognize where I was or whom I was with. I spent much time daydreaming about my parents' death and planning how happily I would live with all that freedom. I also wasted a lot of time daydreaming about someone who was going to come and take me away from all the pain and misery in which I was being forced to live. I retreated inside myself even more. I continued this behavior for the next three years until finally I had a nervous breakdown. I did not want to admit even then what was happening to me or what I was doing, so I went on pretending that nothing was wrong with me. I tried to continue to live a normal life, avoiding as much thinking and talking about my problems as I possibly could. At this time I lost all faith and hope in my religion and in any higher power.

To get away from problems I believed my parents were causing for me, I left home, trying to escape their rules and regulations and looking for love and understanding from other people. All their suggestions for me to seek help were ridiculous as far as I was concerned. I knew there was nothing wrong with me; it was all their fault. So I left home seeking this love and understanding from others and two months later became pregnant. It was necessary for me to get financial assistance from my parents during my pregnancy, so I moved home again. During my pregnancy, I spent some time in a mental institution. At the time the child was born, I felt I was being forced to give him up for adoption. So in my anger and revenge, I tried to kill myself. I also wasn't feeling too good about myself because I had refused to let the father of the child have him. I tried to stab myself to death and found that too painful. Then I thought about downing a bottle of aspirin but I was sure I would get sick, vomit, and suffer before I would die. So instead I decided to try to get pregnant again—while drinking away my pain.

I found a man with whom I lived for the next year and a half who beat me up repeatedly. I drank continuously, ate compulsively, and submitted to a great deal of sex that was painful, degrading, and physically quite harmful. It was a vicious circle which led me nowhere except deeper into self-pity, and contempt for myself and others. After a time, I became terribly frightened and sick of it, so I ran away.

I went back and lived with my parents. I thought I would try to straighten out my life and get back on the "right path." I quit drinking, went on crash diets, had no sexual relations, and merely sat around licking my wounds. After about six months of this, I became restless and bored, so I ran back to the excitement of my other way of life. I started working two jobs and going to night school because of my boredom. In my spare time I would walk the streets getting picked up by any man who would buy me a drink or spend some time with me. I met a man in this way whom I lived with and started the same pattern of behavior again: overeating, continuous drinking, beatings, degrading sex, and so forth. I even got to a point in my fear and anger of taking a gun and almost killing him. I continued like this for about a year during which time I lost three jobs due to my irresponsibility — going to work drunk, missing work, and so on. I was fired from one job because I was too ashamed to tell my boss that I had been raped and that is why I was all beaten up. Instead I let him believe it was my fault. I didn't ever try to stand up for myself because I didn't believe I was worth it.

Again I ran home to my parents. I only lasted a week before I became restless and left again. For the next two years I replaced most of my relationships with people with drugs and food. I used speed, acid, mescaline, cocaine, and marijuana. I had found a new way to try and escape from myself. Through this period, I became more and more paranoid and distrustful of all the people around me. I believed this world was really hell and there was no way I could stand any more pain and suffering. I believed I was the only person who cared about the state of the world and I would some day save everyone — if I felt like it. I spent a lot of time wishing to die, and hating different groups of people whom I judged to be wrong. I started stealing money and food from a church that I worked at. I was arrested twice. I kept having a lot of physical problems, but I would not go to a doctor long enough to find out what was wrong. I freeloaded food and chemicals from people. I was just totally hopeless about life and the world. I associated with inferiors just so I wouldn't be confronted with my behavior. If anyone cared enough to be concerned, I left.

I became scared enough of what I was doing with the drugs, that I quit using them and transferred my dependency to booze and a new relationship. I began living and sleeping with a woman, because I thought this was the answer to all of my problems. In an attempt to try to control and change her, I tried to kill myself again. I failed again, so I took her and almost totally withdrew into isolation and dependency. I rejected all the people I had previously known and did little else outside my home besides going to work. I knew from the time I met her that I did not love her, but I used and misused myself and her as I had done in the past. In my depression and despair, after over four years of this I left her and proceeded to do everything in my power to tell her and show her that it was all her fault for my unhappiness.

It took me a couple of days to get into another relationship which I thought was completely different from the ones of the past. It took me a month to admit that it was exactly the same, and at that point I feel I hit bottom. I had nowhere else to go and nothing left to try. I had been through everything I knew of, and finally realized that I didn't know anything I needed to know about how to take care of myself and how to live. I had been to several different sensitivity groups, support groups, and therapy groups and thought these had taught me all I needed to know about myself. But where were they now? How come I felt worse than I ever had in my whole life?

One of the women I had gone with previously began attending a Twelve-Step Program for herself. I became resentful and jealous — why should she get help, why should everyone care so much about her when I was the one who was "wronged?" About that same time I started looking at the patterns of my own behavior. I realized that my relationships involved excessive drinking, physical abuse, sex without love or caring, and overeating. I very seldom had a sense of humor about anything anymore; everything always had to be deadly serious. Almost everyone I have ever known I have ended up disliking or hating, or never liked in the beginning. I used to believe I was a poor misunderstood soul who had so much love and goodness to give to others but no one was good enough or smart enough to want it. So I always went away.

At first when I started admitting these things I again tried to convince myself that everyone else was sick and needed help. Because I needed someone to talk to so desperately, I started attending Al-Anon meetings (I was going to help out my friends in AA). I only remained there a couple of months before I admitted that a lot of my rationalizations and righteousness about my behavior were just a bunch of bull. At this point I finally had the good sense to admit to myself that I was very deluded and had been for a very long time.

I came into Emotions Anonymous in November of 1975, and my life has not been the same since. After all these years and all these problems and pain that I had made for myself, I felt I was completely alone. I allowed myself to trust no one and to have no faith or belief in any power greater than myself. Through the EA Program I now have that belief, and the belief in the support of the people who care about me.

Some of the areas which Emotions Anonymous has taught me to look at in myself are taking responsibility for myself and my own behavior, and not blaming other people, places, or things for my problems. I have seen through EA that to hold onto my hatred, resentments, and fears is only hurting me. I have also seen that when I have been hurt by someone, I usually tried to hurt someone else in return.

When I first came into Emotions Anonymous, I learned that I can be happy even though I am not perfect. I was taught to begin looking for my happiness and contentment within myself instead of from other people, places, or things. I've learned I can only control my own behavior and not everyone around me as I have tried to do so often.

I have begun to accept myself for who I am and to work on changing those things about me that I wish changed. It is very hard and painful at times, and yet I see a lot more strength in myself than I believed I had in the past. To me, the most important thing I have learned is to take care of myself — the following are some the the areas in which I have begun to do that.

Due to my bad relationships with men in the past, my fear and hatred of them, the rape, the beatings, and the sex, I see I have used these experiences to feel sorry for myself and to hate all men. I eventually had begun to hate all women too. I have just completed a treatment program in which I have learned to look honestly at myself as a woman and a lesbian, and at my anger and rage. I now have a way of dealing with these emotions instead of by killing someone else or myself with chemicals, anger, or food.

All of my life I have misused and abused myself with compulsive overeating and eating junk food. I feel very bad about myself when I do, and the extra weight I gain helps to feed my physical and emotional problems. I am now in Overeaters Anonymous and working my food program for myself. I have also lost fifty pounds through the Program.

I used drugs and alcohol because I was shy and I could let go and do some things I thought I wanted to do while taking no responsibility for my behavior. I used to escape myself and my feelings. I have just completed two treatment programs for my chemical dependency, which taught me a lot about my responsibility to myself and how to get back in touch with those feelings.

I used sex for trying to control and possess another person without having to spend time or energy to love anyone. During those three years I spent being sexual with men, I was not able to get pregnant, but I did manage to get gonorrhea. Because of it and the painful sex, and because I took so little care of myself physically, two years ago it was necessary for me to have a hysterectomy. I am now taking care of my body by being aware of what is going on with it and seeing a doctor when it is necessary. I am also in a program at the University to help me change my attitudes about myself sexually.

I used work because that was the only way I could feel good about myself — by what I could accomplish, not by who I am. I used work as an escape from finding out who I was, what I wanted, what I liked; as an escape instead of relaxation and recreation. I now exercise regularly, play volleyball, and dance. I see that I need a lot of relaxation and recreation along with my work to be healthy and happy.

Through Emotions Anonymous I have learned to recognize these changes I needed to make in my life for my own happiness. I've just begun. I have a lot more that I want to do for myself. The most valuable thing I have gotten from EA through the Twelve Steps and the support of the people, is the courage to find out who I am. For me that is a matter of doing anything and everything that will teach me how to be more honest with myself and how to take care of myself.

I love all of you.

Diane

(30)
KEY TO SERENITY

I'm Nancy and I'm powerless over my feelings of inferiority and hypersensitivity. That statement, and the full acceptance of it, by me, is the "key" to enter the shelter of Emotions Anonymous. Because I was raised in a conservative, reserved, perfectionistic German family, the expression of feelings of pain and loneliness was not allowed and was even criticized as weak, foolish, and wrong. "Don't act like a baby." "You shouldn't feel that way." "That's ridiculous." Those are just a few examples of statements I'd heard many times throughout the formative years of my life.

I was the oldest and only girl in a family of four children and received much harrassment from my younger brothers and father. My father never had a sister, his mother was mentally ill, and the German culture then placed a low value on the female. Because of my hypersensitivity, I felt things more acutely than others, and experienced tremendous pain from the men in my life. I found at a very early age that food was a way for me to feel good and relieve my pain. Needless to say, I soon found myself a "fatty." The kids used to tease me. I still remember a good friend of my mother's telling her, in front of me, laughing, how she was wondering how many months pregnant I was because of my round, fat tummy. It wasn't long before I felt ashamed of me, and I was sure that the whole world also felt that way about me.

My adolescence was filled with more memories of fear, pain, and loneliness. I was shy, withdrawn, and very uncomfortable with people. I just kept on eating. Fortunately, my intelligence helped, because I desperately wanted

231

approval and school seemed to be the only place where I did excel. Church was helpful, too, because there were kind, accepting people there. I belonged to the choir and youth group. At that time in my life, I found much strength from my relationship with God. Due to the desperate desire to be wanted and accepted, I made a decision, very early in junior high school, to make a career in the helping professions my goal. I not only wanted to feel good about myself but also, due to my own deep pain, wanted to help others find help, hope, and an end to the kind of suffering I had experienced.

I attended the University and in my freshman year met my husband-to-be on a blind date (naturally). He, too, was overweight and came from an unhappy family. He was the first boy I'd ever dated more than twice. His sense of humor and sense of abandon were good for me. I guess we both needed something and clung to each other. His mother had never really given him much love, and I felt great compassion for him in his lonely home environment. My need to help him and his need for a mother brought us to marriage about two years later. Our parents had wanted us to wait, but our need was greater. Our marriage was stormy. We were possessive, demanding, and extremely immature in every way. I cut short my education, and in three years became a mother.

After fourteen years, one more child, three major separations, and numerous short-term breaks, my husband and I found EA. I truly consider this a miracle. Two very extremely emotional and not especially compatible people are still married and reasonably happy. My husband has lost sixty pounds since joining EA, and I am finally in control of my eating, at my normal weight, and holding!

When I was still embarrassed about having to admit that I was powerless over my emotions, I discovered my intelligence had little to do with it. I had gone back to the University during my last separation in an attempt to fulfill my childhood dream, and studied psychology and various forms of therapy. I had read it all!! None of my studies had been able to give me the "key" to this serenity and peace of mind. I'd even worked in a medical clinic with a counselor and saw many people each day receive help openly. From my childhood learning, I still felt stupid, weak, and inferior because I couldn't handle myself better. Even when our marriage improved, with the help of the counselor where I had worked, I still felt unhappy, bored, and restless. I had gone back to school, was now attending weekly EA meetings, and had lost all of the weight I had gained.

But life was still empty for me! I attended church each week and occasionally felt at peace there. I found, though, that once back home it soon disappeared. I'd tried an affair of sorts long ago, but found the reality unsatisfactory in that type of relationship and knew that I couldn't turn in that direction anymore. While separated I had tried sex, and discovered that this, too, only lasted until the next morning. I went into depression. I used to think that the perfect man would fill this emptiness. This erroneous thinking led me to many infatuations with men with whom I had strong feelings of sexual attraction. Even though I didn't become physically involved with these men, the thoughts about them became obsessive. I felt frustrated and trapped in my marriage.

During this phase of my life when the marriage was improving, and other major problems were solved, my search for meaning continued. I tried to lose myself in hobbies and materialism. Funds limited these rapidly! I smoked marijuana and tried to work myself away from my misery. Physical limitations and my strong responsibility to my children soon stopped both of these escapes. After joining EA I soon realized that these were only temporary answers, and I knew better than to continue to use them. They really didn't work anyway, for very long.

I'd been groping for about six months when I finally hit my bottom point. I cried out, "Is this all there is?" I finally admitted to myself and to the EA people that I just couldn't struggle anymore. Life just had to be more than being straight with sex, food, and being free of obsessions. I should be finding some contentment and peace once in awhile.

In EA I heard others tell how they each had made a decision to turn their will and life over to the care of God as they understood Him. I asked myself where had my God gone and when. I didn't really know. After moving away from the church of my childhood and trying many churches, I'd lost God. My shyness prevented me from becoming involved, as I had been once, and my many marital problems made me feel ashamed. I'd hidden from people, especially those in the church.

I don't know how long I stumbled before I decided to gamble. I finally let go and let a Higher Power, whatever that was I wasn't sure, try to help. Those other people seemed to think it helped, so why not? Suddenly, the light began to shine! I could finally see and experience that glorious secret, serenity. I was with all of those beautiful people. I basked in the love, the warmth, and the blessed serenity.

Today, this twenty-four hours, I'm practicing the Twelve Steps. I still find it hard to admit I need help (Step One), and ask for it. Today I feel alive! I feel that my life is worth something! I feel joy! I feel love!!

The people in EA are holders of the valuable secret of life. They have discovered truth, in their own way. The truth found in all the ancient wisdom and world religions. They are willing to tell about themselves at their weekly meetings. People of all ages, sizes, shapes, professions, and backgrounds can be found there. There are no leaders because everyone shares the work to maintain the Program. No one is forced into the Program. A person must really want the secret bad enough to work for it. Each person must find his own way to work each of the Twelve Steps.

I am grateful for all of the pain I've suffered. I am even more determined to continue toward my goal of helping other suffering people. Whenever I struggle and stumble, I know that all I have to do is ask for help. I can now dare to dream and set goals, with the help of my Higher Power. Every day I can accept reality and the little irritations because of the hope I've found. Even though I can still quickly find myself slipping back, I don't panic anymore! I know that Emotions Anonymous is not far away, and always waiting for me.

Nancy

(31)

GETTING TO KNOW ME!

I'm Diana. I am powerless over my emotions. Two years ago I came into Emotions Anonymous. The Twelve-Step Program has brought me an inner peace I would not have believed humanly possible. I would like to share with you part of my life which goes back to my search for serenity.

I was one of four children. My father is an alcoholic. When I was five months old my mother gave me to my dad's parents to raise. I was used as a pawn to get money for my father's drinking. If he wanted money and his mother refused to give it to him, he would take me home with him until Grandma would give in to him.

As a young child I can remember his drunkenly setting me in the back of his pickup and taking me out to the farm. Many terrifying memories followed. When we got to the farm he forced my brother to drink beer until he was so intoxicated he fell off the porch. He then became angry with my mother, broke her nose, and she fell unconscious. When she came to, she took a beer bottle, broke it, and hit him in the face. These became common events in the years to follow. My parents separated for good when I was five. My sister and brother came to live with my grandparents and my dad lived with his mother until her death. Today my brother is an alcoholic. My sister has suffered from severe emotional problems.

I was to become my father's scapegoat. I was always an an extremely shy and sensitive child. I don't know if I would have had problems or not, but as a result of my environment and because of who I am, my emotional problems started very young. My search for God and serenity started as far back as I can remember.

My father's violence got progressively worse. I began to live in terror. In addition to his cruelty to me, my brother, and my sister, it wasn't uncommon for him to beat his mother up. After one event, my grandma ended up in the hospital with a heart attack.

By the time I was a teenager I was a mess. To complicate things, I'm part Indian and being the daughter of the town drunk didn't help. In school kids were unkind to me, I used to be called names and on a few occasions was even spat upon. My self-esteem dropped lower and lower. I didn't have love or acceptance at home or in society.

When I was sixteen years old I quit school. That spring I met my husband. He couldn't believe the events that had taken place in my life. He asked me to marry him. So three months before my seventeenth birthday, I became a wife. Nine months and nine days later I became a mother. Thirteen months later I had my second baby. So there I was, eighteen, a mother of two children, and a mess!

When I was twenty-one, I started having nightmares about my childhood, my stomach ached, and inside I felt a great loneliness. This was to be the beginning of trying to find out who I was and where my God was.

I then decided to go to a psychiatrist. I wanted to go back to school but I was too insecure. I feared failure. I was too shy to do the things a normal person takes for granted. Simple things like singing in a choir, going to school, being active in social events, all of these things I found hard to do. The psychiatrist said, "The more you go out into society, the more at ease you will become. Someday it will be natural to you and you will be comfortable." Not so! Yes, I learned to function out there but I didn't lose my shyness. I never lost the feeling of being different, deep in my gut which asked, "Why me, God?"

Then I started to search for myself. I read every self-help book I could find. I tried applying their principles, but I could not lose that empty feeling. I searched for serenity. I thought if I could use a little more will power I could help myself.

All of a sudden, I was in my thirties. I had not lost the empty feeling and I began to be afraid. I really disliked myself for not having been able to overcome my insecurities and shyness. I began to focus on my shyness. For me to be thirty-three with the thought of having to function in society without being able to overcome or accept my problems, really upset me. I must add, when I was quite young, I learned to hide my insecurities. If I couldn't overcome them, I would hide them until I could overcome them. Around my gut-level friends and family I'm neither shy nor insecure!

A little over two years ago I read "I Ain't Much Baby, But I'm All I've Got," inquired about EA and my life began to change. For the first time I could accept my shyness and insecurities.

Because of my shyness I will always have a harder time functioning in society. Because of who I am, I've become very selective of my environment. I very carefully weed out what's important to me and my family, and the rest I leave to those of you out there who can do the things that make me a wreck!

I have learned if I force myself to do things because other people expect them, I suffer in the end. When I do things that feel right for me, I think I am a better person. I try to live "one day at a time."

Sometimes I still feel like the kid nobody wanted. Sometimes I still feel that great emptiness within me, but that's okay. It will pass. I'm still just as shy and insecure as I ever was, but most of the time I can accept it.

At long last my search for serenity has ended. Through the Twelve Steps of EA I have found the tools to live a full life. Serenity isn't bells ringing, it's not fireworks, it is a quietness within myself. I thank God for the Twelve-Step Program, for without it I would just be existing.

I tried for thirty-three years to help myself and what I've discovered is "I need my Higher Power!" I couldn't do much on my own. I needed to hand it over and let God take it. God gave me this new life - He gave me the tools to use, but He leaves the choice of using them up to me!

I would like to share with you how my life has been since joining EA. Before I came into EA, I was a very sensitive person. I am still sensitive, but through the Program I've come to see my sensitivity as a character defect. It has caused me a lot of unhappiness over the years which often led to depression. Since joining EA, I have only had one bad depression.

EA has helped me to become a better wife, mother and friend. It used to be if someone was unkind to me it could ruin a day for me. Obviously, if it ruined my day, it also ruined my family's day because a depressed person certainly doesn't emit any "good feelings."

I never really saw myself as a self-centered person, but I now realize if I hadn't been self-centered I couldn't have been hurt so much. I sure must have been thinking of myself a lot or I wouldn't have ended up depressed so often.

I probably hurt myself the most. The Program has taught me that I have a choice to be miserable or to work at not being miserable. Before I came into EA, I thought my past was behind me, but that my reactions were a result of my past. Through the Program I've learned to live one day at a time, so I can keep old reactions in perspective and choose which way I wish to react.

Before coming to EA I never realized what high expectations I had of those close to me. Because of my sensitivity I judged my family by my standards. My sensitivity doesn't make me any greater or lesser than others. I sometimes find it difficult to be accepting of aggressive personalities. EA has helped me to be more tolerant of others. People have a right to be who they are. If I can't handle the situation it is best for me to avoid it but I don't sit in judgment.

Through the Program I have come to see myself for what I am, the good and the bad. I can only give what I am today. Some people may not want what I can give, but that's okay, as I don't always want what others can offer me. We all are so different and yet so much alike.

With the tools of the Twelve-Step Program I'm working to improve my life. It isn't always easy to look at ourselves. A lot of us, I am sure, have gone through pain in our lives and sometimes it's easy to get bogged down with our emotions. However, when we hurt enough we have to re-evaluate our lives.

I am just a "babe" in EA. There is so much I still have to learn. It will take a lifetime to really know and accept myself and learn to take life as it comes, but the rewards from this Program make it all worthwhile.

For me the Twelve-Step Program is my life.

Diana

APPENDICES

I.

THE TWELVE SUGGESTED
STEPS OF EMOTIONS
ANONYMOUS®

1. We admitted we were powerless over our emotions — that our lives had become unmanageable.
2. Came to believe that a Power greater than ourselves could restore us to sanity.
3. Made a decision to turn our will and our lives over to the care of God *as we understood Him.*
4. Made a searching and fearless moral inventory of ourselves.
5. Admitted to God, to ourselves and to another human being the exact nature of our wrongs.
6. Were entirely ready to have God remove all these defects of character.
7. Humbly asked Him to remove our shortcomings.
8. Made a list of all persons we had harmed, and became willing to make amends to them all.
9. Made direct amends to such people wherever possible, except when to do so would injure them or others.
10. Continued to take personal inventory and when we were wrong promptly admitted it.
11. Sought through prayer and meditation to improve our conscious contact with God *as we understood Him*, praying only for knowledge of His will for us and the power to carry that out.
12. Having had a spiritual awakening as the result of these steps, we tried to carry this message, and to practice these principles in all our affairs.

Reprinted through the permission of
A.A. World Services, Inc.

II.

THE TWELVE TRADITIONS OF
EMOTIONS ANONYMOUS®

1. Our common welfare should come first; personal recovery depends on EA unity.

2. For our group purpose there is but one ultimate authority — a loving God as He may express Himself in our group conscience. Our leaders are but trusted servants; they do not govern.

3. The only requirement for EA membership is a desire to become well emotionally.

4. Each group should be autonomous except in matters affecting other groups or EA as a whole.

5. Each group has but one primary purpose — to carry its message to the person who still suffers from emotional problems.

6. An EA group ought never endorse, finance, or lend the EA name to any related facility or outside enterprise, lest problems of money, property, and prestige divert us from our primary purpose.

7. Every EA group ought to be fully self-supporting, declining outside contributions.

8. EMOTIONS ANONYMOUS® should remain forever non-professional, but our service centers may employ special workers.

9. EA, as such, ought never be organized; but we may create service boards or committees directly responsible to those they serve.

10. EMOTIONS ANONYMOUS® has no opinions on outside issues, hence the EA name ought never be drawn into public controversy.

11. Our public relations policy is based on attraction rather than promotion; we need always maintain personal anonymity at the level of press, radio, and films.

12. Anonymity is the spiritual foundation of our traditions, ever reminding us to place principles before personalities.

III.

HELPFUL CONCEPTS OF THE EA PROGRAM

1. We come to EA to learn how to live a new "Way of Life" through the Twelve-Step Program of Emotions Anonymous which consists of: Twelve Steps, Twelve Traditions, Concepts, Serenity Prayer, Slogans, Just for Todays, EA literature, weekly meetings, telephone and personal contacts, and living the Program one day at a time. We do not come for another person — we come to help ourselves and to share our experiences, strength and hope with others.

2. We are experts only on our own stories, how we try to live the Program, how the Program works for us, and what EA has done for us. No one speaks for Emotions Anonymous as a whole.

3. We respect anonymity — no questions are asked. We aim for an atmosphere of love and acceptance. We do not care who you are or what you have done. You are welcome.

4. We do not judge — we do not criticize — we do not argue. We do not give advice regarding personal or family affairs.

5. EA is not a sounding board for continually reviewing our miseries, but a way to learn to detach ourselves from them. Part of our serenity comes from being able to live at peace with unsolved problems.

6. We *never* discuss religion, politics, national, or international issues, or other belief systems or policies. EA has no opinion on outside issues.

7. EMOTIONS ANONYMOUS® is a spiritual Program, not a religious Program.

8. The Steps suggest a belief in a Power greater than ourselves — "God as we understand Him." This can be human love, a force for good, the group, nature, the universe, or the traditional God (Deity), or any entity a member chooses for his/her Higher Power.

9. We utilize the Program — we do not analyze it. We have not found it helpful to place labels on any degree of illness or health.
10. We may have different symptoms, but the underlying emotions are the same or similar. We discover we are not unique in our difficulties and/or illnesses.
11. Each person is entitled to his own opinions and may express them (within the precepts of EA) at a meeting. We are all equal — no one is more important than another.
12. Part of the beauty and wonder of the EA Program is that at meetings we can say anything and know it *stays there.* Anything we hear at a meeting, on the telephone, or from another member is confidential, and is not to be repeated to anyone — EA members, mates, families, relatives, or friends.

IV.

JUST FOR TODAY
(I Have a Choice)

1. JUST FOR TODAY I will try to live through this day only, not tackling my whole life problem at once. I can do something at this moment that would appall me if I felt that I had to keep it up for a lifetime.

2. JUST FOR TODAY I will try to be happy, realizing that my happiness does not depend on what others do or say, or what happens around me. Happiness is a result of being at peace with myself.

3. JUST FOR TODAY I will try to adjust myself to what is — and not force everything to adjust to my own desires. I will accept my family, my friends, my business, my circumstances as they come.

4. JUST FOR TODAY I will take care of my physical health; I will exercise my mind; I will read something spiritual.

5. JUST FOR TODAY I will do somebody a good turn and not get found out — if anyone knows of it, it will not count. I shall do at least one thing I don't want to do, and I will perform some small act of love for my neighbor.

6. JUST FOR TODAY I will try to go out of my way to be kind to someone I meet; I will be agreeable; I will look as well as I can, dress becomingly, talk low, act courteously, criticize not one bit, not find fault with anything, and not try to improve or regulate anybody except myself.

7. JUST FOR TODAY I will have a program. I may not

follow it exactly, but I will have it. I will save myself from two pests — hurry and indecision.

8. JUST FOR TODAY I will stop saying, "If I had time." I never will "find time" for anything. If I want time I must take it.

9. JUST FOR TODAY I will have a quiet time of meditation wherein I shall think of God *as I understand Him*, of myself, and of my neighbor. I shall relax and seek truth.

10. JUST FOR TODAY I shall be unafraid. Particularly, I shall be unafraid to be happy, to enjoy what is good, what is beautiful, and what is lovely in life.

11. JUST FOR TODAY I will accept myself and live to the best of my ability.

12. JUST FOR TODAY I choose to believe that I can live this one day.

THE CHOICE IS MINE!

V.

SLOGANS WE USE

1. Let go and let God.

2. You are not alone.

3. Easy does it.

4. Live and let live.

5. First things first.

6. Look for the good.

7. But for the Grace of God.

8. Know thyself — be honest.

9. This too shall pass.

10. I need people

11. **Four A's**
    a. Acceptance
    b. Awareness
    c. Action
    d. Attitude

12. I have a choice.

VI.

HOW TO GET IN TOUCH WITH
EMOTIONS ANONYMOUS

Any two or three persons gathered together for emotional health may call themselves an EA chapter provided that as a group they have no other affiliation.

If you cannot find EA in your locality, you may write: Emotions Anonymous International, P.O. Box 4245, St. Paul, Minnesota 55104, and this office will assist you in locating the nearest group. If there is no group in your area, they will assist you in starting a group.

God, grant me the serenity
To accept the things I cannot change
Courage to change the things I can
And the wisdom to know the difference.

VII.

EMOTIONS ANONYMOUS LITERATURE

The EA Pamphlet — You Are Not Alone

Enormity Of Emotional Illness

Chart of Emotional Illness & Recovery

Know Thyself, Be Honest

Inventory Wallet Card

I Have a Choice (wallet card)

* * *

EA Magazine, "Carrying the EA Message"
Yearly bound copies available from January
for the previous five years

* * *

Introduction to Children's EA

Children's EA Pamphlet

Introduction to Youth EA

EMOTIONS ANONYMOUS LITERATURE – Continued

Guide For Forming and Conducting New and Existing Groups of EA

Suggested Format For Meetings

Emotions Anonymous Meeting Sign

Meeting Table Card

Treasurer's Weekly Record Form

Group Inventory

Guide For Local Answering Service

Sample News Release

* * *

World Directory

(Confidential for EA members & groups only)

* * *

Introduction to Loner's EA

Loner Or New EA Groups Wishing a Sponsor

Suggestions For Sponsoring A Loner In Loner's Emotions Anonymous

Suggestions For Sponsors Of New Or Loner EA Groups

LEA Questionnaire

– NOTES –

– NOTES –

– *NOTES* –